great fast food

great fast food

EBURY PRESS
LONDON

First published in Great Britain in 2000

9 10 8

Copyright © Eaglemoss Publications Ltd 2000
Gary Rhodes original recipes © Gary Rhodes 2000
Front cover photograph of Gary Rhodes: Sian Irvine.
Front cover (top right): Eaglemoss Publications/
William Lingwood; (centre right): Eaglemoss Publications/
Ken Field; (bottom right): IPC Syndication/
Options Magazine/James Merrell.

First published by Ebury Press
Random House, 20 Vauxhall Bridge Road,
London SW1V 2SA

Random House Australia (Pty) Limited
20 Alfred Street, Milsons Point, Sydney, New South Wales
2061, Australia

Random House New Zealand Limited
18 Poland Road, Glenfield, Auckland 10, New Zealand

Random House South Africa (Pty) Limited
Endulini, 5A Jubilee Road, Parktown 2193, South Africa

The Random House Group Limited Reg. No. 954009

www.randomhouse.co.uk

A CIP catalogue record for this book is available
from the British Library.

ISBN 0 09 187900 0

This book was designed, edited and produced by
Eaglemoss Publications Ltd, based on the partwork
Good Cooking with Gary Rhodes

Printed and bound in Italy by De Agostini

contents

introduction

For most of us, time always seems to be in short supply. Our days are spent juggling tasks, deciding what must be done and what can be left undone. In a busy lifestyle, time spent in the kitchen may seem like a luxury few can afford. But preparing delicious meals doesn't have to be a chore. With Great Fast Food you can now rustle up a quick lunch for the family or a spontaneous supper for friends, knowing that the one thing you haven't scrimped on is taste.

Great Fast Food is packed with 200 mouth-watering recipes specially selected to be as simple and speedy as possible – all you need is a well-stocked store cupboard and a few carefully chosen fresh ingredients. Try them out and discover how easy and enjoyable it is to create delicious dishes even if you have only half an hour.

As time is tight and searching for the 'right' recipe could have you giving up in despair and telephoning for a costly takeaway, I've arranged the recipes in handy groups: Soups & Salads; Lunches & Snacks; Main Meals; Pasta, Rice, Noodles & Polenta and Hot & Spicy.

To make things even simpler, each of the five sections is further divided into Chicken & Meat, Fish & Shellfish and Vegetarian.

There's no need to worry about wasting hours searching for the elusive or exotic as all the ingredients used in the recipes can be found in larger supermarkets. If a particular ingredient is unusual or out of season, I've given suitable alternatives.

So why not join me in proving that good, tasty home-cooked food doesn't have to cost a fortune or take forever!

Gary Rhodes

essential information

kitchen safety

- Put chilled and frozen foods into your fridge or freezer as soon as possible after purchase.
- Keep raw meat and fish at the bottom of your fridge.
- Keep the coldest part of your fridge at 0-5°C.
- Wash fresh produce before preparation.
- Prepare and store raw and cooked food separately.
- Clean work surfaces, chopping boards and utensils between preparing food which is to be cooked and food which is not.
- If you are pregnant or elderly, avoid food that contains raw eggs.
- Check *use by* dates on packaging and keep to them.
- If re-heating food, make sure that it's piping hot.
- Always wash your hands before preparing or handling food.
- Keep pets away from worktops and food dishes.

notes on the recipes

- Measurements are given in both metric and imperial: do not mix the two.
- Spoon measurements are level.
- Tbsp and tsp are used for tablespoon and teaspoon: tbsp means 15ml, tsp means 5ml. An accurate set of measuring spoons helps to avoid mistakes.
- Season, unless otherwise stated, means seasoning with salt and freshly ground black pepper.
- Eggs are size 2 (large).
- Ingredients are listed with the most important first, then other ingredients in the order of use.

oven temperatures

Celsius	Fahrenheit	Gas	Description
110°C	250°F	$1/4$	Cool
120°C	250°F	$1/2$	Cool
140°C	275°F	1	Very low
150°C	300°F	2	Very low
160°C	325°F	3	Low
170°C	325°F	3	Moderate
180°C	350°F	4	Moderate
190°C	375°F	5	Moderately hot
200°C	400°F	6	Hot
220°C	425°F	7	Hot
230°C	450°F	8	Very hot

stock

Two simple meaty stocks – one brown, one white – a vegetable stock and a fish stock are must-haves for successful cooking. It's well worth making a batch once a month or so and freezing it in the amounts needed for your favourite recipes. Stocks keep for two months in the freezer. However, if you haven't the time or have run out, you can buy some good alternatives. The 284ml (10fl oz) tubs of ready made beef, lamb, chicken, fish and vegetable stocks found in the chill cabinets of most large supermarkets are nearly as good as home-made. They have authentic colours and flavours. Stock cubes are the third option. Look out for salt-free cubes or dissolve them in slightly more boiling water than recommended – twice the amount for fish stock cubes – to reduce the saltiness.

soups and salads

20 mins

vietnamese chicken noodle soup

serves 4

500g (1lb 2oz) chicken, skinned, boned and diced

1 litre (1¾ pints) chicken stock

4 tbsp Thai fish sauce

1 tbsp grated ginger

350g (12oz) rice noodles

50g (1¾oz) beansprouts

60g (2¼oz) onions, finely sliced

2 tbsp chopped fresh Thai or ordinary basil

2 tbsp chopped fresh coriander

2 tbsp chopped fresh mint

2-4 bird's-eye red chillies, deseeded and finely sliced

2 spring onions, finely sliced

1 lime, quartered, to serve

1 Place the chicken, stock, fish sauce and ginger in a large pan and bring to the boil. Cover and simmer for 10-15 minutes or until the chicken is cooked.
2 Meanwhile, boil a kettle of water and soak the noodles according to the packet instructions.
3 Drain the noodles and divide them between 4 serving bowls. Divide the cooked chicken between the bowls and add the beansprouts and onions. Sprinkle with the chopped basil, coriander and mint.
4 Pour the chicken broth into the bowls and then scatter the chillies and spring onions over the top.
Serve with the lime wedges.

pancetta, gnocchi & tomato soup

30 mins

serves 4

125g (4½oz) diced pancetta
250g (9oz) fresh gnocchi
300ml (10fl oz) passata
25g (1oz) butter
2 large onions, sliced
1 garlic clove, crushed
125ml (4fl oz) dry white wine
1 red pepper, deseeded and diced
1 yellow pepper, deseeded and diced
1.2 litres (2 pints) chicken stock
2 tbsp pesto
55g (2oz) parmesan, grated
salt and pepper
1 tbsp pinenuts, toasted
sprigs of fresh basil, to garnish

1 Melt the butter in a large saucepan over moderate heat and cook the onions, pancetta and garlic for 5 minutes until the onion is just softened. Add the wine, bring to the boil and simmer until the wine has reduced by about one-third.
2 Stir in the peppers, stock and passata and return to the boil; simmer for 15 minutes. Add the gnocchi and bring back to the boil for 3 minutes. Stir in the pesto and parmesan and season to taste. Simmer for 1 minute until the cheese has melted.
Serve in individual bowls, sprinkled with the pinenuts and garnished with the basil.

20 mins

creamy pea soup with crispy bacon

serves 4

450g (1lb) frozen peas

25g (1oz) butter

1 large onion, finely chopped

450ml (16fl oz) vegetable or chicken stock

pinch of sugar

salt and pepper

150ml (5fl oz) single cream

6 rashers of smoked streaky bacon, cut into fine strips and fried until crisp

1 Melt the butter in a large saucepan, add the onion and cook for 2-3 minutes until softened. Pour in the stock and bring to the boil.

2 Add the peas and sugar, bring back to the boil and simmer for about 3 minutes. When the peas are tender, season with salt and pepper.

3 Blitz in a liquidizer or with a hand blender until the soup is smooth. (For a super-smooth texture, push the soup through a sieve.) Add the cream and heat gently.

Serve with a dash of cream swirled in the centre and sprinkle with crispy smoked bacon.

Tip For a fresh taste, add a sprig of mint to the stock while cooking and serve with a scattering of finely chopped chives.

20 mins

vegetable soup with cheddar & bacon

serves 4

350g (12oz) cauliflower florets

350g (12oz) leeks, trimmed and sliced

350g (12oz) potato, diced

140g (5oz) mature cheddar, grated

150g (5½oz) smoked bacon, chopped

1 tsp grated nutmeg

salt and pepper

850ml (30fl oz) chicken or vegetable stock

300ml (10fl oz) milk

1 tbsp English mustard

grated cheddar to garnish

1 Bring the stock to boil in a large saucepan. Add the cauliflower, leeks, potato, nutmeg and seasoning. Cover and boil for 15 minutes until the vegetables are tender.

2 Place the bacon pieces in a frying-pan and dry-fry until crispy. Set to one side.

3 Pour the vegetables and stock in a blender and blitz until smooth. Pour back into the saucepan and stir in the milk, mustard and cheddar. Check the seasoning and bring to a simmer.

Serve the soup garnished with bacon and grated cheese.

Tip If you make the soup ahead to freeze it, leave out the cheese. Before use, thaw it and bring to the boil then add the cheese and garnish as above.

20 mins

grilled chicken & mixed bean salad

serves 4

4 chicken breasts

420g (15oz) can mixed beans, drained and rinsed

1 red chilli, deseeded and finely sliced

3 spring onions, finely chopped

zest and juice of 2 limes

½ cucumber, peeled and diced

1 avocado, peeled and diced

6 tbsp olive oil

1 tbsp chopped fresh coriander

oil for frying

juice of 1 lemon

salt and pepper

good-quality mayonnaise

1 Mix together the beans, chilli, onions, lime zest and juice, cucumber, avocado, olive oil and coriander and season with salt and pepper.
2 Brush a grill pan or frying-pan with a little oil and lemon juice. Heat until it smokes then add the chicken breasts.
3 Cook for about 8 minutes on each side. If the chicken breasts are quite thick, you may have to cook them for a little longer.
Serve the chicken warm with a portion of the bean salad and a large dollop of good-quality mayonnaise.

warm chicken goujon salad

25 mins

serves 4

4 chicken breasts, cut in strips

25g (1oz) plain flour

salt and pepper

55g (2oz) sesame seeds

115g (4oz) breadcrumbs

2 eggs, beaten

oil for shallow-frying

1 tbsp sesame oil

225g (8oz) baby spinach leaves, washed

2 tbsp dark soy sauce

1 tsp Thai chilli dipping sauce

2 oranges, segmented

1 Sprinkle the flour on to a plate and season. Turn the chicken strips in the flour, coating well, then set aside.

2 Mix the sesame seeds and breadcrumbs in a small bowl. Dip the coated chicken in the beaten egg, then toss in the breadcrumb mixture.

3 Heat the oil in a wok or large frying-pan and fry the chicken in batches (5 minutes for each batch) until crisp and golden. Drain on kitchen paper and keep warm.

4 Heat the sesame oil in a separate pan. Add the spinach, soy sauce and Thai sauce and cook for 1 minute until the spinach is wilted. Quickly add the orange segments and stir in, then add the chicken. Toss and serve.

Serve the salad on warm plates, with hot chilli sauce.

15 mins

chicken salad with strawberries

serves 4

2 x 100g (3½oz) packets sliced smoked chicken
280g (10oz) strawberries, hulled
2 tbsp raspberry vinegar
2 tbsp groundnut oil
1 tsp Dijon mustard
salt and black pepper
2 avocados
1 mini cucumber
25g (1oz) watercress

1 Put 115g (4oz) strawberries in a food processor with the raspberry vinegar, oil and mustard; season to taste. Blitz until the strawberries are puréed.

2 Peel, stone and slice the avocados and divide between 4 individual serving bowls. Slice the cucumber and the remaining strawberries and add to the bowls.

3 Add the watercress and smoked chicken slices to the bowls and mix together. **Serve** drizzled with the strawberry vinaigrette and seasoned with freshly ground black pepper.

Tip Strawberries may seem an unusual ingredient for a savoury dish but their freshness works well with the other flavours. In fact, in times past it was quite common to serve strawberries sprinkled with a little pepper.

30 mins

duck, shallots & garlic salad

serves 4

4 duck breasts, skinned

8 shallots, peeled and halved

12 garlic cloves, unpeeled

5 tbsp olive oil

115g (4oz) spinach leaves, washed and stalks removed

3 tbsp hazelnut oil

2 tbsp raspberry vinegar

salt and pepper

1 Heat 2 tbsp olive oil in a frying-pan and sauté the shallots and garlic over a low to medium heat for 7-10 minutes.

2 In a separate frying-pan, cook the duck on a high heat for 7-8 minutes, turning once until the duck is browned but still pink in the middle.

3 Arrange the spinach leaves on 4 plates.

4 Whisk the remaining olive oil with the hazelnut oil and raspberry vinegar. Season the dressing well.

5 Cut the duck breasts in thin slices. Arrange on the spinach leaves and scatter the shallots and garlic on top.

Serve the salad with the dressing drizzled all over.

Tip You can use the shallots, onions and salad with different warm meats. Try stir-fried chicken livers, or strips of chicken breast, turkey breast or pork.

20 mins

celeriac, ham & cheese salad

serves 4

375g (14oz) celeriac, ready shredded

225g (8oz) ham or smoked pork loin, cut in thin strips

200g (7oz) gruyère cheese, cut in thin strips

175ml (6fl oz) good-quality mayonnaise

2 tsp Dijon mustard

2 heaped tbsp drained caper berries, sliced, plus 8 reserved as a garnish

2 tbsp finely chopped flatleaf parsley

5 tbsp single cream

lettuce leaves and chopped parsley to garnish

1 Mix the mayonnaise with the mustard, sliced capers, parsley and cream in a bowl.
2 Toss the celeriac with the strips of ham and cheese. Then add the dressing and mix well.
Serve on a bed of lettuce and garnish with parsley and caper berries.

Tip You can buy shredded celeriac from some supermarkets. Otherwise you can shred it using a food processor or grater.

25 mins

avocado with bacon & spinach

serves 4

2 avocados, peeled and sliced

6 streaky bacon rashers

175g (6oz) baby spinach leaves, washed

4 tbsp crème fraîche

2 tbsp olive oil

zest and juice of 1 lemon

1 garlic clove, crushed

salt and pepper

fresh crusty bread to serve

1 Dry-fry the bacon in a small frying-pan until crispy. Take the rashers out of the pan and pat off any remaining fat with kitchen paper.

2 Mix together the crème fraîche, olive oil, lemon zest and juice and the garlic. Season to taste.

3 Add the avocado to the spinach leaves and toss in the crème fraîche dressing. Crumble the crispy bacon into the salad.

Serve the salad with fresh crusty bread.

Tip To create a vegetarian version of this dish, substitute crunchy toasted pecan nuts for the crisp bacon pieces. Roasted peanuts or roasted cashews are equally acceptable replacements. Use salted or unsalted nuts to suit your own taste and adjust the seasoning accordingly.

thai-style beef salad

15 mins

serves 4

500g (1lb 2oz) rump steak, thinly sliced

350g (12oz) Little Gem lettuce leaves, shredded

175g (6oz) cucumber, peeled and diced

2 medium carrots, peeled and grated

115g (4oz) fresh beansprouts

2 tsp vegetable oil

1 garlic clove, crushed

1 tsp finely chopped lemon grass stalk

2 tbsp lime juice

2 tbsp finely chopped coriander

2 tbsp finely chopped basil

2 tbsp olive oil

1 tbsp sweet chilli sauce

1 Arrange the lettuce, cucumber, carrots and beansprouts on a serving dish.
2 Heat the vegetable oil in a wok or deep frying-pan. Gently fry the garlic and lemon grass for 30 seconds.
3 Add the beef, turn up the heat and stir-fry for 1-2 minutes. Remove the beef and place on top of the lettuce and vegetables.
4 Add the lime juice to the pan with the coriander, basil, olive oil and sweet chilli sauce.
5 Cook the sauce, stirring well, for about 1 minute. Then pour over the beef.
Serve with little bowls of sweet chilli sauce.

smoked cod chowder

30 mins

serves 4

225g (8oz) smoked cod

600ml (20fl oz) milk

1 large white potato, peeled and cubed

1 bay leaf

5 peppercorns

25g (1oz) butter

3 spring onions, chopped

1 red pepper, diced

1 x 200g (7oz) can sweetcorn, drained

1 tbsp fresh coriander, chopped

300ml (10fl oz) good-quality fish stock

salt and pepper

1 Put the cod, milk, potato, bay leaf and peppercorns into a large frying-pan and bring to the boil. Reduce the heat and simmer for 10 minutes or until the potato is soft.

2 Strain the milk into a jug and reserve. Skin the fish and flake the flesh. Mash the potato until smooth.

3 Heat the butter in a large saucepan and cook the spring onions and red peppers until softened. Add the reserved milk, sweetcorn, two-thirds of the chopped coriander and fish stock, bring to the boil and simmer for 5 minutes.

4 Stir in the mashed potato and flaked fish. Season with pepper and cook for another minute.

Serve with the remaining chopped coriander scattered on top and crusty bread on the side.

30 mins

spicy mediterranean seafood soup

serves 4

250g (9oz) seafood mix

2 tbsp olive oil

2 garlic cloves, crushed

2 tsp pimentón

½ tsp chilli powder

780g (1lb 11oz) jar fish soup

200ml (7fl oz) fish stock

100g (3½oz) arborio rice

300g (10½oz) cod, cut into large chunks

chopped flatleaf parsley, to garnish

1 In a large heavy-based saucepan, heat the oil and gently fry the garlic for about 30 seconds.

2 Add the pimentón and chilli powder and fry for another 30 seconds. Pour in the fish soup and stock.

3 Bring to the boil, add the rice and simmer for 12 minutes until the rice is almost cooked.

4 Add the cod and simmer for 3 minutes. Then add the seafood mix and simmer for 5 minutes until the seafood is heated through.

Serve with the flatleaf parsley sprinkled over the top.

Tip Good-quality jars of fish soup are sold in delicatessens and large supermarkets.

mussel, crabmeat & prawn soup

30 mins

serves 4

1kg (2lb 4oz) live mussels, cleaned

150g (5½oz) fresh or canned white crabmeat, drained

200g (7oz) peeled cooked prawns

1 garlic clove, unpeeled

1 shallot, roughly chopped

150ml (5fl oz) dry white wine

300ml (10fl oz) skimmed milk

35g (1¼oz) butter

35g (1¼oz) plain flour

450ml (16fl oz) fish stock

strips of zest and juice of 1 lemon

2-3 tbsp chopped fresh dill

60g (2¼oz) fromage frais

sprigs of dill, to garnish

1 Put the mussels, garlic, shallot and wine in a large pan and cover. Cook over high heat for 6-8 minutes, shaking the pan until the mussels open.

2 Strain, reserving the cooking liquor. When cool enough to handle remove the mussels from their shells, discarding any that have not opened, and reserve. Top the cooking liquor up to 600ml (20fl oz) with the milk.

3 Melt the butter in a large pan and stir in the flour. Mix in the milky liquor and fish stock. Stir and simmer for 5 minutes.

4 Add the crab, mussels and prawns, lemon juice and half the zest. Season with pepper and heat through gently for 3 minutes. Stir in the chopped dill and fromage frais.

Serve garnished with sprigs of dill and remaining lemon zest.

25 mins

beans, artichoke & anchovy salad

serves 4

85g (3oz) block of parmesan cheese

450g (1lb) French beans, trimmed

420g (15oz) can borlotti beans

150g (5oz) artichoke hearts in olive oil, quartered if large

6 tbsp olive oil

2 tbsp red wine vinegar

50g (2oz) can anchovy fillets in oil, drained and halved lengthways

1 Cook the French beans in salted boiling water for 2 minutes. Drain and refresh under cold water. Place in a large bowl with the borlotti beans and artichoke hearts.

2 Mix the oil and vinegar and toss with the salad. Scatter anchovies through the salad.

3 Using a swivel-style potato peeler, shave thin curls from the block of parmesan on to a non-stick baking tray. Cook in a hot oven for 3 minutes until melted and golden. Leave to cool and harden. **Serve** the salad with the parmesan crisps sprinkled on at the last minute.

Tip Use only a non-stick baking tray or one lined with baking parchment or a Teflon-coated sheet as the melted cheese sticks like glue to anything else.

tuna niçoise with balsamic dressing

30 mins

serves 4

4 tuna steaks

75ml (2½fl oz) balsamic vinegar

225g (8oz) new potatoes, skins left on

125g (4½oz) fine green beans

4 shallots, chopped

150ml (5fl oz) olive oil

300g (10½oz) plum tomatoes, peeled, deseeded and diced

a few pitted black olives

3 hard-boiled eggs, shelled and quartered

12 thin slices French bread

1 Pre-heat the oven to 225°C/425°F/gas 7. Boil the potatoes until tender; drain and set aside. Blanch the beans for 2 minutes. Drain and then refresh under cold running water; set aside.

2 Meanwhile, make the dressing; put the shallots, vinegar and 85ml (3fl oz) oil in a pan and cook over low heat for 10-15 minutes until the shallots have softened and browned. Leave to cool.

3 Mix the potatoes, beans, tomatoes, olives and eggs in a bowl. Lightly brush one side of each slice of bread with some oil and toast in the oven until crisp; cool. Add to the bowl.

4 Heat a griddle pan over high heat. Lightly brush the tuna with some of the remaining oil and cook on the griddle for 2-3 minutes on each side.

Serve the salad on individual plates, topped with the tuna and drizzled with some of the shallot dressing.

15 mins

prawn & grapefruit salad

serves 4

20 fresh king prawns, heads removed

2 pink or ruby grapefruit, segmented

2 tbsp vegetable oil

4 tbsp olive oil

2 tbsp lime juice

salt and pepper

200g (7oz) mixed salad leaves

bunch of fresh coriander leaves

1 Heat the vegetable oil in a large frying-pan or wok. Once the oil has started to smoke, add the prawns and stir-fry for 2-4 minutes until pink on the inside, singed on the outside.

2 Whisk the olive oil and lime juice together and season well. Remove the prawns from the pan and mix in a salad bowl with the grapefruit segments. Toss with the lime dressing.

3 Divide the salad leaves between 4 plates. Spoon the prawns and grapefruit on to a bed of lettuce.

Serve with a few coriander leaves on top.

lobster & fennel salad with rocket

30 mins

serves 4

2 x 750g (1lb 10oz) cooked lobsters

1 large head fennel

115g (4oz) rocket leaves

125ml (4fl oz) extra virgin olive oil

2 tbsp lemon juice

1 garlic clove, crushed

1 tbsp capers

1 tsp sugar

2 thyme sprigs, bruised

salt and pepper

2 tbsp chopped dill

parmesan shavings to garnish

1 Trim the fennel head and discard the outer layer. Cut into wafer thin slices and place in a shallow dish.

2 Mix the olive oil, lemon juice, garlic, capers, sugar and thyme together and season. Pour over the fennel. Toss well to coat and leave to marinate for 10 minutes.

3 Cut each lobster in half lengthways and remove the stomach sacs (found just below the eyes). Lift out the tail meat, chop and reserve. Crack open the claws with a mallet and extract the meat.

4 Strain the fennel, reserving the dressing. Arrange it on individual plates with the rocket leaves. Top each salad with the meat from half a tail and meat from a claw.

5 Stir the chopped dill into the reserved dressing, pour over each salad and garnish with parmesan shavings.

Serve with fresh crusty bread.

oriental hot-sour mushroom soup

15 mins

serves 4

1 bunch spring onions

1 large carrot

85g (3oz) mangetout

115g (4oz) yellow oyster mushrooms

55g (2oz) button mushrooms

1 tsp vegetable oil

1 small red chilli, sliced

1cm (½in) piece fresh root ginger, peeled and grated

1 garlic clove, sliced

1.3 litres (2¼ pints) vegetable stock

2 tsp dark soy sauce

1 tbsp white wine vinegar

4 whole star anise

1 Halve the spring onions lengthways then cut into 2.5cm (1in) lengths. Cut the carrot into matchstick-sized pieces. Thinly slice the mangetout lengthways. Split the oyster mushrooms into smaller pieces. Slice the button mushrooms.

2 Heat the oil in a saucepan. Add the spring onions and carrots and fry for 2 minutes. Stir in the mangetout, chilli, ginger and garlic and fry for another 2 minutes.

3 Add the stock and bring to the boil. Stir in the oyster and button mushrooms, soy sauce, vinegar and star anise. Heat gently for 5 minutes. **Serve** piping hot with extra soy sauce on the side.

cauliflower & sweet pepper soup

30 mins

serves 4

450g (1lb) cauliflower florets

1 green pepper, quartered

1 yellow pepper, quartered

115g (4oz) shallots, peeled and quartered

2.5cm (1in) piece of fresh root ginger, crushed

600ml (20fl oz) water

2 tsp salt

425ml (15fl oz) skimmed milk

juice of 1 lemon

4 tsp white wine vinegar

fresh parsley sprigs to garnish

1 Pre-heat the grill to high. Line the grill pan with foil and place the peppers on it, skin side up. Take 2 small florets of cauliflower and place them beside the peppers.

2 Grill for 4 minutes until skin is slightly charred. Cut two of the yellow pepper quarters into strips and set aside. Peel off the skins from the rest of the yellow and green peppers and roughly chop the flesh.

3 Place the shallots, the rest of the cauliflower, the ginger, peppers, water and salt in a large saucepan. Bring to the boil, cover and simmer for 20 minutes.

4 Put the vegetables and cooking liquid in a blender and blitz until smooth. (You may need to do this in several batches.) Return to a clean saucepan and whisk in the milk, lemon juice and vinegar.

Serve hot or cold, garnished with the reserved grilled cauliflower florets, pepper strips and parsley sprigs.

30 mins

mild spiced carrot & parsnip soup

serves 4

500g (1lb 2oz) carrots, peeled and diced

600g (1lb 5oz) parsnips, peeled and diced

1 tbsp olive oil

55g (2oz) butter

1 onion, finely chopped

1 apple, peeled and diced

zest of 1 orange

1 tbsp medium curry paste

2 tsp ground coriander

2 tsp ground cumin

½ tsp turmeric

1.2 litres (2 pints) vegetable stock

½ tsp garam masala

150ml (5fl oz) single cream

1 onion, sliced in rings

croûtons to serve

1 Heat oil and half the butter in a large pan. Add vegetables and apple. Fry gently for 15 minutes until tender.

2 Add the zest, curry paste, coriander, cumin and turmeric. Cook over a high heat for 1 minute, stirring continuously.

3 Add three-quarters of the vegetable stock and bring to the boil. Simmer for 7 minutes.

4 Blitz in a liquidizer or with a hand blender. If it's too thick add the remaining stock.

5 Heat the rest of the butter in a small frying-pan; add the onion rings. Fry until browned.

6 Return the soup to the pan and stir in the garam masala and cream.

Serve the soup garnished with onion rings and croûtons.

30 mins

traditional mulligatawny soup

serves 4

1 medium potato, diced
1 large carrot, diced
1 large onion, chopped
1 leek, cleaned and sliced
2 celery sticks, sliced
25g (1oz) butter
1 tbsp medium curry powder
1 tsp tomato purée
1 litre (1¾ pints) vegetable stock
salt
1 hard-boiled egg, chopped
2 tbsp chopped fresh chives

1 Melt the butter in a large pan. Add the vegetables and cook for 5 minutes. Add the curry powder and cook for a further 2 minutes.
2 Add the tomato purée and the stock. Bring the soup to a simmer, then cover and cook for 20 minutes, until the vegetables are tender.
3 Blitz the soup with a hand blender or in a liquidizer until smooth and season with salt.
Serve garnished with hard-boiled egg and a sprinkling of chives.

Tip Serve the soup with poppadums and cooked long-grain rice for an authentic Anglo-Indian meal. Stir in mango chutney for extra flavour.

20 mins

mexican bean soup with salsa

serves 4

2 x 220g (8oz) cans spicy refried beans

2 tbsp olive oil

2 onions, chopped

2 garlic cloves, crushed

600ml (20fl oz) vegetable stock, made with 2 stock cubes

2 large tomatoes

1 small avocado

½ small red onion

2 tbsp finely chopped fresh coriander

juice of ½ lime

salt and black pepper

4 tbsp soured cream, to serve

1 Heat the oil in a large saucepan and fry the onion and garlic for 10 minutes until golden. Stir in the stock and the beans and cover. Simmer the soup for 5 minutes.

2 Pour the soup into a food processor and blend to make a smooth purée.

3 To make the salsa, finely chop the tomatoes, avocado and red onion and place in a bowl. Add the coriander and lime juice to the bowl and season to taste. Mix well. **Serve** topped with the salsa and 1 tsp of soured cream.

Tip Spicy refried beans in cans are a useful quick ingredient. They already have spices added, but if you like your soup a little hotter, just add some chilli powder to taste.

20 mins

greek-style salad with lemon & mint

serves 4

300g (10½oz) couscous
finely grated rind and juice of
1 lemon
3 tbsp chopped fresh mint
plus a few sprigs for garnish
125ml (4fl oz) olive oil
115g (4oz) pitted black
olives, quartered
140g (5oz) cherry tomatoes,
quartered
140g (5oz) feta cheese, diced
salt and pepper

1 Place the couscous in a large mixing bowl and pour over 400ml (14fl oz) boiling water. Cover with a sheet of plastic wrap and leave to soak for 15 minutes.
2 Meanwhile, for the dressing, whisk the olive oil, lemon juice and half the rind together. Add the mint and season with salt and pepper.
3 When the couscous is softened, fluff it up with a fork. Toss the olives, tomatoes, feta cheese and dressing into the couscous.
Serve garnished with fresh sprigs of mint and lemon zest.

Tip Bulghur wheat makes a delicious alternative to couscous. Either way, this salad goes well with barbecued chicken or fish.

20 mins

broccoli & radicchio salad with blue-cheese dressing

serves 4

675g (1½lb) broccoli florets

250g (9oz) radicchio heart, washed and coarsely chopped

175g (6oz) Roquefort cheese

125ml (4fl oz) olive oil

7 sun-dried tomatoes, bottled in olive oil

2 tbsp balsamic vinegar

4 tbsp single cream

1 Cook broccoli for 1 minute in salted, boiling water. Drain and refresh under cold water. Place the florets in a bowl.

2 Heat 2 tbsp olive oil in a frying-pan and cook the radicchio for 1-2 minutes until just wilted. Add the vinegar at once and allow to cool a little before adding to the broccoli.

3 Meanwhile, slice the sun-dried tomatoes into strips, then mix with the broccoli and radicchio. Crumble in half of the cheese.

4 Mash the rest of the cheese and whisk in the remaining olive oil and cream. Pour the dressing over the salad.

Serve the salad divided between 4 bowls with warm French bread on the side.

Tip The Roquefort dressing tastes just as good poured over a fresh mixed leaf salad.

25 mins

quail eggs, mushroom & potato salad

serves 4

12 quail eggs

250g (9oz) mushrooms

400g (14oz) new potatoes

7 tbsp olive oil

2 tbsp balsamic vinegar

1 garlic clove, crushed

salt and pepper

100g (3½oz) salad leaves

1 Cook the potatoes in salted boiling water for 10 minutes until tender. Drain and halve.
2 Heat 3 tbsp olive oil in a frying-pan. Fry mushrooms for 3-4 minutes. Add 1 tbsp vinegar, then transfer to a salad bowl. Wipe out the pan.
3 Heat 3 tbsp olive oil in pan, season and fry potatoes for 5 minutes. Add garlic and fry for 2 minutes. Put in salad bowl.
4 Heat rest of oil in pan, add the eggs and cook for 2 minutes. Transfer to a plate covered with kitchen paper.
5 Toss the potatoes and mushrooms in the bowl with the remaining balsamic vinegar. **Serve** with the fried eggs on top and season to taste.

Tip Quail eggs are difficult to crack because they're so small. Make a cut in the shell with a serrated knife, then slip the contents into the pan.

15 mins

ricotta & bean salad with olive oil

serves 4

350g (12oz) ricotta cheese

750g (1½lb) fresh broad beans, in their pods

115g (4oz) frozen peas

175g (6oz) small radishes, trimmed and halved

55g (2oz) black olives

small bunch fresh mint

4 tbsp extra virgin olive oil

4 tbsp balsamic vinegar

ciabatta loaf, sliced and toasted to serve

1 Pod the broad beans and blanch them in salted boiling water for 2 minutes. Drain, reserving the liquid, then refresh the beans under cold water. Peel off the waxy grey outer skins.

2 Cook the peas in the reserved liquid for 5 minutes. Drain and refresh under cold water.

3 Cut the ricotta into thick slices. Place on individual plates and divide the beans, peas, radishes and olives between them. Roughly tear the mint leaves and scatter over each plate.

4 Mix together the olive oil and balsamic vinegar, then drizzle a little over each salad. Season to taste.

Serve with the slices of toasted ciabatta.

Tip Use feta cheese as an alternative to ricotta for a sharper flavour.

30 mins

baby vegetable salad with herb mayonnaise

serves 4

1kg (2lb 4oz) mixed baby vegetables and salad leaves

2 egg yolks

2 tsp Dijon mustard

1 tsp caster sugar

1 tbsp white wine vinegar

4 tbsp mixed fresh herbs

salt and pepper

300ml (10fl oz) light olive oil

capers and cocktail gherkins to garnish

1 From the mixed vegetable pack, choose those that are best eaten cooked and blanch for 1-2 minutes. Trim and wash the rest.

2 Arrange the blanched and raw vegetables and the salad leaves on a large platter.

3 Place the egg yolks, mustard, sugar, vinegar and herbs in a blender and blitz until the mixture is creamy.

4 With the motor running, add the olive oil slowly in a thin stream, making a thick mayonnaise. Taste and adjust seasoning if necessary.

5 Continue to blend until the mayonnaise becomes a vivid green colour.

Serve the herb mayonnaise in a separate dish and garnish the salad with capers and cocktail gherkins.

Tip If the mayonnaise becomes too thick at any stage, you can whisk in 1-2 tbsp boiling water to thin it down a little.

15 mins

tomato, mango & coriander salad

serves 4

500g (1lb 2oz) plum
tomatoes, cut into quarters

500g (1lb 2oz) yellow and red
cherry tomatoes, halved

1 small ripe mango, peeled
and cubed

small bunch fresh coriander

4 spring onions, sliced

small bunch fresh purple basil

1 tbsp sesame seeds, toasted

4 tbsp extra virgin olive oil

1 tbsp lime juice

1 garlic clove, crushed

1 tsp chopped stem ginger

2 tsp ginger syrup

salt and pepper

1 Arrange the plum tomatoes
and cherry tomatoes on a
plate. Spoon the mango over
them.

2 Scatter the spring onions,
coriander, basil and sesame
seeds over the salad.

3 Whisk or blitz the oil, lime
juice, garlic, ginger and syrup
together until you have a
smooth dressing.

Serve the salad with the
dressing drizzled over and
season lightly.

Tip Purple basil is also
known as opal
basil and has a
slightly more muted
flavour than ordinary basil.
It gives the salad an
amazing colour lift.

15 mins

tricolore salad with pesto dressing

serves 4

2 avocados, halved, peeled and diced

4 plum tomatoes, peeled and sliced

115g (4oz) yellow and red cherry tomatoes, halved

6 sun-dried tomatoes, chopped

2 tbsp chopped fresh basil plus a few leaves for garnish

1 garlic clove, crushed

½ tbsp pinenuts

25g (1oz) parmesan cheese, grated

4 tbsp olive oil

115g (4oz) mozzarella, diced

1 To make the pesto dressing, put the chopped basil, garlic, pinenuts, parmesan and olive oil in a food processor and blitz until smooth.

2 Arrange the different types of tomato on a plate. Top with the diced avocado and the cubes of mozzarella. Spoon over the dressing.

Serve garnished with fresh basil leaves.

Tip Sun-blush tomatoes make a lush alternative to sun-dried ones. They are only half-dried and are therefore more tender and juicier than their wrinklier relatives. You'll find them on the deli counters of large supermarkets.

citrus couscous salad

30 mins

serves 4

225g (8oz) couscous

2 tomatoes

2 oranges

6 tbsp olive oil

2 tbsp chopped fresh parsley

2 tbsp chopped fresh mint

1 garlic clove, crushed

1 red onion, diced

juice of 1 orange

juice of 1 lime

salt and pepper

sprig of mint, to garnish

1 Put the couscous in a bowl with 425ml (15fl oz) boiling water; set aside for 5 minutes.
2 Meanwhile, pour boiling water on the tomatoes and set aside for 1 minute. Peel, then deseed and dice.
3 Peel the 2 oranges and divide into segments.
4 When the couscous has absorbed the water, fork the grains apart and mix in the oil, herbs, garlic, onion, tomatoes and orange and lime juices. Stir in the orange segments; season to taste. Set aside to cool for about 20 minutes to allow the flavours to develop. **Serve** garnished with a sprig of mint.

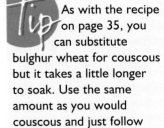

Tip As with the recipe on page 35, you can substitute bulghur wheat for couscous but it takes a little longer to soak. Use the same amount as you would couscous and just follow the packet instructions.

chinese-style warm salad

30 mins

serves 4

280g (10oz) tofu, cubed

3 tbsp sherry

2 tbsp soy sauce

juice of 1 lime

1 garlic clove, crushed

115g (4oz) shiitake mushrooms, halved

1 red pepper, deseeded and sliced

1 bunch spring onions, cut into long, thin strips

175g (6oz) beansprouts

3 tbsp olive oil

1 tbsp sesame oil

1 tbsp honey

2 tbsp lemon juice

lettuce leaves to serve

1 Pre-heat the grill to high. Combine the sherry, soy sauce, lime juice and garlic in a bowl. Add the tofu and mushrooms and marinate for 10 minutes.

2 Drain off the marinade and save for later. Spread the mushrooms and tofu on a baking tray and grill for 10 minutes until golden, basting occasionally with the reserved marinade.

3 Meanwhile, mix the pepper, spring onions and beansprouts in a large bowl. To make the dressing, whisk the olive oil, sesame oil, honey and lemon juice together in a small bowl.

4 When the mushrooms and tofu are cooked, add them to the bowl. Pour the dressing over the salad and toss well. **Serve** the salad at once on a bed of lettuce leaves.

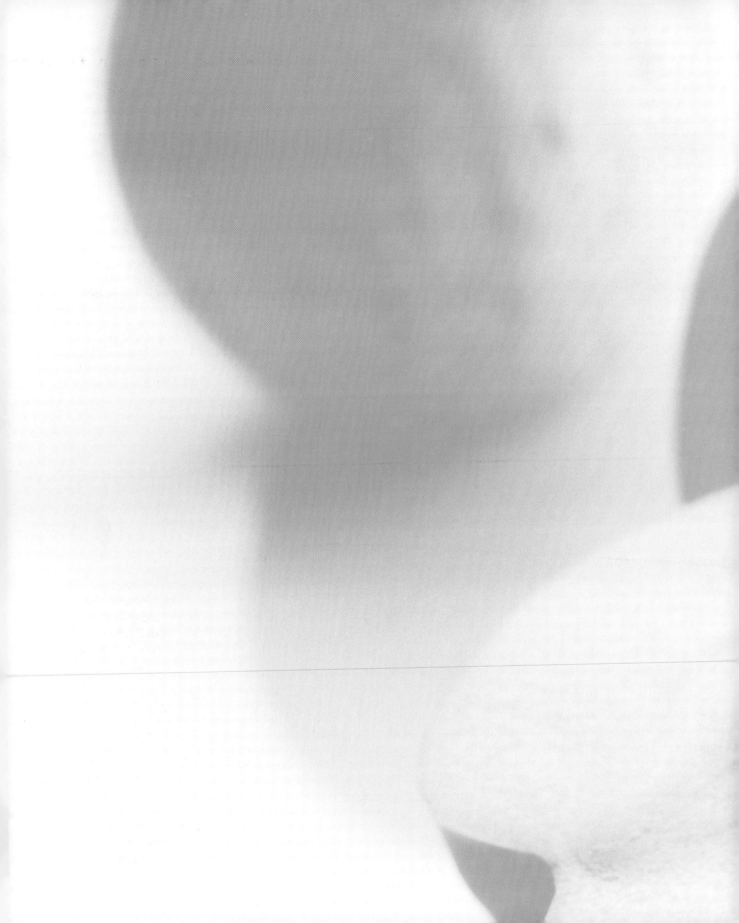

lunches
and
snacks

20 mins

savoury chicken mini vol-au-vents

serves 4

16 ready-cooked mini vol-au-vent cases

2 chicken breasts, cut in strips

150ml (5fl oz) dry white wine

2 tbsp lemon juice

115g (4oz) potatoes, peeled and cubed

115g (4oz) young asparagus, cut in 2.5cm (1in) lengths

8 tbsp good-quality mayonnaise

2 tbsp crème fraîche

parsley sprigs to garnish

1 Pre-heat the oven to 170°C/325°F/gas 3. Place the vol-au-vent cases on a baking tray and warm in the oven for 20 minutes.

2 Pour the white wine and lemon juice into a saucepan and bring to the boil. Poach the chicken strips in the wine for 10 minutes.

3 Bring a small pan of salted water to the boil and add the potato. Boil for 5 minutes then add the asparagus and boil for a further 3 minutes.

4 Drain the potatoes and asparagus. Remove the chicken strips with a slotted spoon. Place the potatoes, asparagus and chicken in a bowl and add the mayonnaise and crème fraîche. Stir well until everything is well coated.

5 Distribute the mix between the vol-au-vent cases.

Serve 4 vol-au-vents per person for nibbles or a starter and garnish each one with parsley sprigs.

25 mins

melting chicken ciabatta

serves 4

115g (4oz) taleggio cheese, sliced

4 chicken breasts, thinly sliced

4 large pieces ciabatta

1 tbsp sunflower oil

2 tsp Chinese five-spice powder

4 plum tomatoes, sliced

115g (4oz) rocket leaves

4 tbsp olive oil

1 tbsp lemon juice

salt and pepper

1 Pre-heat the grill to high. Place the chicken strips in a bowl and rub in the sunflower oil and spices.

2 Place under the grill for 10 minutes until cooked through.

3 Slice open the ciabatta pieces and toast the insides under the grill. Once toasted, divide the sliced tomato, taleggio cheese and chicken between four halves of ciabatta and top with the other four halves.

4 Grill the filled ciabatta for 2 minutes on each side then cut each piece in two.

5 Toss the rocket leaves with the olive oil and lemon juice and season.

Serve 2 pieces of ciabatta per person with a little rocket salad.

30 mins

crispy chicken drumsticks

serves 4

8 chicken drumsticks, skins on

55g (2oz) plain flour

salt and pepper

2 eggs, beaten

1 tsp paprika

85g (3oz) fine fresh white breadcrumbs

oil for deep-frying

salad leaves, to serve

lemon wedges, to serve

1 Sprinkle the flour on a plate and season. Dust the chicken drumsticks with the flour, then coat well with the beaten egg.

2 Mix the paprika with the breadcrumbs and season. Use to coat the drumsticks. Pack on any remaining breadcrumbs in a second layer.

3 Heat the oil in a deep-fat fryer or deep frying-pan. Test the temperature with a piece of bread – if it turns golden brown within 2 minutes, it is ready. Add the drumsticks, 4 at a time, and deep-fry for 8-10 minutes until golden and crisp.

4 Drain on kitchen paper and keep warm.

Serve with salad leaves and lemon wedges.

Tip For a slightly chunkier, more rustic texture, use granary or wholemeal breadcrumbs. These breadcrumbs will be slightly larger than the white version, so press them very firmly on to the chicken drumsticks.

10 mins

cold turkey with tuna mayonnaise

serves 4

900g (2lb) cold cooked turkey breast, thickly sliced

75ml (2½fl oz) dry white wine

200g (8oz) can of tuna, drained

250g (9oz) mayonnaise

5 anchovies, rinsed

2 tbsp capers, rinsed

juice of ½ lemon

2 tbsp chopped flatleaf parsley

salt and pepper

sprigs of flatleaf parsley and tarragon to garnish

1 To make the dressing, blend the tuna, mayonnaise, anchovies, 1 tbsp capers and lemon juice in a liquidizer.

2 Add 3-5 tbsp white wine to thin the sauce slightly so that it will pour well over the turkey, then season to taste.

Serve the turkey slices with the sauce spooned over them. Scatter capers and chopped parsley on top and garnish with sprigs of parsley and tarragon. This dish eats particularly well with a green bean and cherry tomato salad.

Tip This simplified version of a classic Italian dish – Turkey tonnato – is an original way of serving cold roast turkey. It's excellent for staving off those 'Oh no, not turkey again!' post-Christmas blues.

30 mins

marinated lamb with aubergine dip

serves 4

350g (12oz) diced lamb

55g (2oz) feta cheese

2 tbsp black olive paste

1 garlic clove, crushed

5 tbsp olive oil

1 red onion, peeled and cut into eighths

pitta bread to serve

fresh mint and lamb's lettuce

for the aubergine dip

450g (1lb) whole aubergines

2 tbsp Greek yoghurt

2 tbsp olive oil

1 garlic clove

1 Pre-heat the oven to 220°C/450°F/gas 7. Rub the aubergine with a little olive oil and bake for 20 minutes.
2 Meanwhile, blend or mash the feta cheese, olive paste, the crushed garlic clove and 3 tbsp olive oil until smooth. Add the lamb and leave to marinate for 10 minutes.
3 Thread the lamb cubes and red onions alternately on to the skewers. Grill or barbecue for 15 minutes until the lamb is cooked.
4 Split the aubergine and scrape the flesh into a sieve; press down to get rid of any bitter juices. Put the flesh in a blender with the garlic, yoghurt and oil. Blitz briefly.
Serve piled into pitta bread with the dip and some lamb's lettuce. Garnish with fresh mint and lamb's lettuce.

Tip Black olive paste is sold in jars in most delicatessens and supermarkets.

simple spanish cold platter

15 mins

serves 4

400g (14oz) Serrano ham, thinly sliced

400g (14oz) spicy chorizo sausage, thinly sliced

400g (14oz) salami, thinly sliced

100g (3½oz) caper berries

400g (14oz) mixed salted almonds, cashews and pinenuts

100g (4oz) jar green olives in brine

100g (4oz) can black olives

100g (4oz) jar green olives

2 tbsp olive oil

1 tbsp lemon juice

4 garlic cloves, crushed

pepper

1 Arrange a mixed selection of the meats on four plates and scatter the caper berries over the top.

2 Divide the nuts between four small bowls.

3 Drain the olives and tip them all into a large bowl.

4 In a small bowl, whisk together the olive oil, lemon juice and garlic and season with pepper.

5 Pour the dressing into the bowl of olives and toss until all the olives are well coated.

6 Share out the olives between four small dishes. Place a bowl of nuts and a dish of olives on each plate beside the meats.

Serve with crusty white bread and a large jug of refreshing chilled sangria.

30 mins

spanish-style tortillas

serves 4

4 small chorizo sausages, sliced

1 tbsp sunflower oil

1 red pepper, deseeded and finely diced

4 spring onions, sliced

6 eggs, beaten

4 tbsp milk

salt and pepper

25g (1oz) butter

4 tortillas

1 Heat the oil in a frying-pan and fry the chorizo, pepper and spring onion for 3-4 minutes until the pepper and spring onion are soft.

2 Meanwhile, whisk together the eggs and milk and season well. Heat the butter in a saucepan and add the eggs. Cook gently, stirring occasionally, until softly scrambled.

3 Mix the cooked chorizo, pepper and spring onion into the scrambled egg.

4 Lay the tortillas out flat and divide the scrambled egg mixture between them.

Serve the tortillas folded over the filling.

Tip Why not try some different fillings for these tortillas? You could keep with tradition and mix grilled bacon and tomatoes with the scrambled eggs. Or you could make it even spicier by frying garlic and chillies with the chorizo, peppers and spring onions.

egg & ham baked in peppers

30 mins

serves 4-5

10 eggs

10 slices dry-cured smoked ham

5 large yellow, orange or red peppers

55g (2oz) butter

salt and pepper

ready-made bread croûtons

salad leaves to serve

1 Pre-heat the oven to 190°C/375°F/gas 5. Bring a large pan of water to the boil.
2 Cut the peppers in half lengthways leaving the stalks on. Remove the seeds.
3 Add the peppers to the pan of boiling water and simmer for 5-8 minutes or until knife-tip tender. Drain well.
4 Grease an ovenproof dish with half the butter. Arrange the peppers in the dish.
5 Fold a slice of ham inside each pepper. Break an egg carefully into each pepper on top of the ham. Season and top each egg with a small knob of butter.
6 Scatter over the croûtons. Set the dish in the oven and bake for 12 minutes until the eggs are just set.
Serve immediately with a side salad.

 For home-made croûtons, cut up white sliced bread into cubes. Heat some oil in a frying-pan. Fry until crispy and golden, turning occasionally.

cheese, ham & spinach gratin

30 mins

serves 4

500ml (18fl oz) ready-made cheese sauce

12 thick slices cooked ham

500g (1lb 2oz) fresh spinach leaves

1 onion, finely chopped

½ tsp ground nutmeg

55g (2oz) parmesan cheese, grated

55g (2oz) fresh breadcrumbs

salt and pepper

55g (2oz) butter

1 Pre-heat the oven to 200°C/400°F/gas 6. Melt the butter in a frying-pan and add the onion. Cook for 2 minutes until slightly softened.
2 In another pan, cook the spinach with a dash of water until it wilts. Squeeze all liquid from the spinach and season with nutmeg.
3 Heat the cheese sauce in a saucepan. Divide the spinach, ham and onion between 4 ovenproof gratin dishes.
4 Pour the cheese sauce over the spinach, ham and onion. Sprinkle the parmesan and breadcrumbs over the top. Place in the oven for 15 minutes. Once bubbling and hot through, place the dishes under the grill for 3 minutes to brown the cheese and breadcrumbs.
Serve the gratin with fresh crusty bread.

25 mins

potato gratin with bacon & sage

serves 4

450g (1lb) potatoes, skins on and thickly sliced

8 rashers bacon, sliced

large bunch of sage leaves

200g (7oz) parmesan cheese, finely grated

55g (2oz) gruyère, finely grated

55g (2oz) butter

1 onion, chopped

2 garlic cloves, crushed

salt and pepper

2 tbsp single cream

1 Pre-heat the grill to high. Cook the potatoes in boiling salted water for 10-12 minutes until tender, then drain.

2 Melt the butter in a large frying-pan. Add the onion and garlic and fry until softened. Add the bacon and cook for 2-3 minutes until crispy.

3 Add the potatoes to the pan and cook for 3-4 minutes turning continuously. Transfer the contents of the pan to an ovenproof dish.

4 Sprinkle the sage leaves on top. Add the cream to the frying-pan and heat while mixing it with the pan juices. Pour over the potatoes.

5 Sprinkle the grated cheeses over the potatoes and season well. Place under the grill for 7-8 minutes until the cheese has lightly browned and the cream has soaked in.

Serve with a selection of sauces, such as tomato sauce and mayonnaise, or topped with fried eggs.

30 mins

american pancakes with bacon & eggs

serves 4

55g (2oz) plain flour

6 eggs

100ml (3½fl oz) milk

500g (1lb 2oz) unsmoked streaky bacon

a little vegetable oil

knob of butter

maple syrup, to serve

1 Pre-heat the grill to high. Sift the flour into a bowl. Beat 2 eggs into the milk and whisk into the flour. Set aside to rest.
2 Grill the bacon until it's crispy. Beat together the remaining eggs.
3 Put a frying-pan over moderate heat. When slightly heated, rub it over with a piece of kitchen paper, dipped in a little oil. Pour in the batter and cook for 6-7 minutes, turning once.
4 Meanwhile, melt the butter in a frying-pan and pour in the eggs. Cook, stirring occasionally, until the eggs are scrambled to your liking.
5 Cut the pancake into quarters and place on individual plates. Divide the bacon between the plates.
Serve with the maple syrup drizzled over the bacon and then topped with the scrambled eggs.

bacon & sweetcorn rösti

25 mins

serves 4

8 rashers bacon, cut into thin strips

200g (8oz) can sweetcorn, rinsed and well drained

4 potatoes, peeled

1 onion

1 beaten egg

salt and pepper

3 tbsp olive oil

½ Savoy cabbage, shredded, to serve

1 Grate the potatoes and onion and, using your hands, squeeze out all the excess liquid. Put in a bowl and stir in half the strips of bacon, the sweetcorn and beaten egg; season to taste.

2 Heat 2 tbsp oil in a large, heavy-based frying-pan. Spoon 4 piles of the rösti mixture into the pan and press each one down, using a spatula. Cook for about 3 minutes on each side until golden brown. Remove from the pan and keep warm.

3 Heat the remaining oil in the frying-pan and add the rest of the bacon; fry until slightly crispy.

4 Meanwhile, steam the shredded Savoy cabbage until just tender.

Serve the shredded cabbage and cooked bacon piled on top of the rösti.

cauliflower cheese with bacon

20 mins

serves 4

300ml (11fl oz) ready-made four-cheese sauce

4 baby cauliflowers

4 rashers streaky bacon, finely diced

5 tbsp vegetable oil

1 tsp dried sage

40g (1½oz) fresh white breadcrumbs

salt and pepper

ground nutmeg

sage leaves to garnish

1 Dry-fry the bacon in a frying-pan until crisp. Add 1 tbsp vegetable oil, the dried sage and the breadcrumbs and continue frying until the crumbs are crisp.

2 Stand the cauliflowers upright in a large pan and pour boiling water over them until it comes a third of the way up them. Sprinkle with salt, cover and simmer for 4-5 minutes. Check to see they are tender with a sharp knife. Drain the cauliflowers.

3 In a small frying-pan, heat the remainder of the oil and add the sage leaves. Fry until crisp then drain on kitchen paper.

4 Pour the sauce into a small saucepan and heat. Season with pepper and nutmeg. Pour a generous amount of the sauce over the cauliflowers. Scatter each serving with crisp bacon and breadcrumbs. **Serve** the cauliflower with crumbled fried sage leaves.

potato & mackerel pasties

30 mins

serves 4

2 x 125g cans (5oz)
mackerel fillets in oil, drained

175g (6oz) canned new
potatoes

3 spring onions

2 tsp Dijon mustard

1 tbsp fresh dill, chopped

375g (13oz) packet
ready-rolled puff pastry

1 egg, beaten

salt and pepper

good-quality mayonnaise

1 Pre-heat the oven to 220°C/425°F/gas 7. Place the mackerel, potatoes, spring onions, mustard and dill in a bowl and mash with the back of a fork. Season with salt and pepper.
2 Roll out the pastry to measure 38cm (15in) square. Cut out four 18cm (7in) rounds. Brush the edges with some of the beaten egg.
3 Place 2-3 tbsp of the fish mixture in the middle of each round. Bring the edges together to form a pasty. Press down all round the edges. Brush the tops of the pasties with the remaining egg and bake in the oven for 15 minutes until golden. **Serve** with a dollop of good-quality mayonnaise.

Tip This is a good way of using up roast, boiled or mashed potatoes. Just substitute them for the canned new potatoes.

30 mins

tacos with tuna & guacamole

serves 4

2 avocados, peeled, stoned and sliced

8 ready-made tacos

2 x 200g (8oz) cans tuna, drained

juice of 2 limes

dash of Tabasco

salt and pepper

1 lettuce (lollo russo), washed

4 radishes, roughly chopped

punnet of cherry tomatoes, halved

½ cucumber, diced

3 tbsp olive oil

juice of 1 lemon

soured cream to serve

1 Pre-heat the oven to 190°C/375°F/gas 5. Place the tacos in the oven to crisp them up.

2 To make the guacamole put the avocado in a bowl with the lime juice and Tabasco. Mash with the back of a fork until thoroughly mixed. Season to taste.

3 Meanwhile, tear the lettuce leaves into bite-sized pieces. Mix the lettuce with the radishes, tomatoes, cucumber, tuna, olive oil and lemon juice. Toss them together lightly and season to taste.

4 Remove the tacos from the oven and put them on the plates. Fill them with the tuna and salad. Spoon a generous amount of guacamole into each taco.

Serve with a bowl of soured cream on the side.

15 mins

sardine & mushroom pâté

serves 4

2 x 120g (4oz) cans sardines in oil, drained

1 tbsp olive oil

150g (5oz) button mushrooms, sliced

375g (13oz) cottage cheese

85g (3oz) cream cheese

juice of 1 lime

salt and pepper

slices of toast

lime wedges, to garnish

crushed black pepper

1 Heat the olive oil in a frying-pan and fry the mushrooms for 5 minutes until golden. Cool a little.

2 Mix the two cheeses in a food processor together with the drained sardines, lime juice and a pinch of salt and pepper.

3 Transfer to a mixing bowl and stir in the mushrooms. **Serve** with plenty of warm toasted bread and garnish with a couple of lime wedges and crushed black pepper.

Tip Chop the mushrooms roughly or keep them whole for extra texture and chunkiness, depending on your own personal taste.

tomato scramble with anchovies

30 mins

serves 4

6 eggs, beaten

4 large tomatoes

25g (1oz) butter

150ml (5fl oz) double cream

salt and pepper

large pinch of ground mace

50g (2oz) can anchovies, drained

1 Pre-heat the oven 200°C/400°F/gas 6.

2 In a bowl, beat the eggs and the cream together, season well and add the mace.

3 Melt the butter in a medium-sized saucepan. Pour the egg mixture into the pan and cook gently over a low heat, stirring all the time, until the eggs are lightly scrambled.

4 Meanwhile, cut the tops off the tomatoes, scoop out the insides and discard. Stand the tomatoes on a greased baking tray and pop them in the oven for 5 minutes.

5 Spoon the creamy scrambled eggs into the tomatoes.

Serve the tomatoes and egg with anchovies on top.

Tip Mace is the skin surrounding the nutmeg kernel. It has a similar but more intense flavour than nutmeg. If you find it hard to get hold of ground mace, you can use nutmeg instead.

25 mins

smoked trout brioche

serves 4

225g (8oz) smoked trout, flaked

4 brioche rolls

8 eggs

salt and pepper

25g (1oz) butter

4 tbsp crème fraîche

2 tbsp chopped chives, leaving a few whole for garnish

1 Pre-heat the oven to 180°C/350°F/gas 4. Cut a thin slice from the top of each brioche roll, scoop out the centre and discard. Place the rolls and their lids in the oven for 10 minutes until crisp.
2 Melt the butter in a saucepan. Beat the eggs together, season and pour into the pan. Cook slowly, stirring all the time, until lightly scrambled. Stir in the crème fraîche, flaked smoked trout and the chopped chives.
3 Spoon into the crispy brioche rolls and replace the lids at a jaunty angle on top. **Serve** garnished with a few chives.

25 mins

salmon & cucumber boats

serves 4

2 mini cucumbers, halved lengthways

115g (4oz) smoked salmon pieces

55g (2oz) cream cheese

dash of Tabasco sauce

2 tbsp freshly chopped dill

pepper

8 cooked tiger prawns

chopped dill to garnish

lime wedges to serve

1 Using a teaspoon, scoop out the seeds from the centre of the cucumbers. Discard the seeds. Turn upside down to drain on kitchen paper.

2 Place all but a few small pieces of the smoked salmon in a food processor with the cream cheese, Tabasco sauce and the dill. Blend briefly for a few seconds until mixed but still fairly chunky.

3 Diagonally slice each cucumber half into 2 pieces widthways. Pile the salmon mixture on to the pieces of cucumber and put two on to each plate. Season with pepper.

4 Finely shred the reserved smoked salmon and top each cucumber piece with some salmon and a prawn.

Serve with more dill sprinkled on top and lime wedges on the side.

Tip If mini cucumbers are unavailable, cut shorter pieces from full length one instead.

25 mins

smoked salmon pastry blinis

serves 4

115g (4oz) smoked salmon

450g (1lb) ready-rolled puff pastry

4 tbsp mascarpone

4 tsp chopped dill

sprigs of dill to garnish

25g (1oz) salmon caviar (optional)

1 lemon, cut in quarters

1 Pre-heat the oven to 220°C/425°F/gas 7.
2 Cut out four 16cm (6¼in) rounds from the sheets of puff pastry. Arrange the bases on a baking sheet and bake in the oven for 15 minutes until well risen and golden.
3 Let the bases cool slightly and then top each one with 1 tbsp mascarpone and 1 tsp chopped dill.
4 Divide the smoked salmon into 4 and arrange on top of the mascarpone. Return to the oven for 2 minutes.
5 Remove from the oven and scatter with sprigs of dill, and salmon caviar if you wish.
Serve with a lemon wedge on the side.

salmon, egg & watercress parcels

20 mins

serves 4

200g (7oz) pack of sliced smoked salmon
3 hard-boiled eggs
25g (1oz) watercress, roughly chopped
250g (9oz) cream cheese
4 tbsp crème fraîche
4 tbsp mayonnaise
zest of 1 lemon
fresh chives, chopped
salmon roe, to garnish
salt and pepper
sliced brown bread, to serve

1 Mix cream cheese, crème fraîche, mayonnaise and lemon zest until smooth.
2 Roughly chop eggs and lightly mix into the cream-cheese mixture with the watercress and most of the chives. Season to taste.
3 Lay 2 long strips of smoked salmon on to the serving plate in the shape of a cross. Place 2-3 tbsp of filling into the middle and draw up the sides of the salmon to form a parcel. Twist the ends to secure. Repeat to form 3 more parcels.
Serve garnished with salmon roe and remaining chives and accompanied with sliced brown bread, lightly buttered.

Tip For a low calorie dish, make the filling from low-fat versions of cream cheese, mayonnaise and crème fraîche.

15 mins

prawns on rye bread

serves 2

200g (7oz) cooked, peeled prawns

4 slices rye bread

3 large sweet cucumbers or large gherkins

3 small cooked beetroots

small bag of salad leaves

3 tbsp olive oil

1 tbsp white wine vinegar

1 tbsp creamed horseradish

1 Lightly toast the rye bread under the grill. Thinly slice the sweet cucumber or gherkins and dice the cooked beetroot.
2 Lay 2 slices of the toasted rye bread on each serving plate. Top each slice with a few salad leaves and divide the prawns, sweet cucumber and beetroot between the slices.
3 Make a dressing by whisking together the olive oil, white wine vinegar and creamed horseradish.
Serve with the dressing drizzled over each open sandwich.

Tip Sweet cucumbers are available in jars and are similar to pickled gherkins – although sweet cucumbers are sweeter and larger.

seafood and feta pouches

30 mins

serves 4

8 sheets filo pastry, cut into
25cm (10in) squares

150g (5½oz) peeled prawns

125g (4½oz) crabmeat

4 tbsp olive oil

1 small onion, chopped

1 small courgette, diced

½ red pepper, chopped

½ carrot, diced

55g (2oz) feta cheese,
crumbled

2 tbsp chopped fresh dill

2 tbsp chopped fresh parsley

1 egg yolk

1 tbsp lemon juice

salad leaves, tomato strips
and rosemary sprigs to garnish

1 Pre-heat the oven to
180°C/350°F/gas 4. Heat
1 tbsp olive oil and gently fry
the onion for 5 minutes. Add
the vegetables and cook for a
further 3 minutes.
2 Combine the vegetables
with the prawns, crabmeat,
feta cheese, dill, parsley, egg
yolk and lemon juice.
3 Lay out 1 square of filo
pastry and brush with olive oil.
Place 2 tbsp of the seafood
mixture in the centre.
4 Draw up the edges and
squeeze together to form a
pouch. Place on a greased
baking tray. Repeat with the
remaining squares of filo pastry.
5 Brush the pouches with
olive oil. Bake for 10-12
minutes until golden brown.
Serve garnished with salad
leaves, strips of tomato and
sprigs of rosemary.

15 mins

grilled green-lipped mussels

serves 4

20 green-lipped mussels, opened and cleaned

85g (3oz) fresh white breadcrumbs

25g (1oz) freshly grated parmesan

juice and grated zest of 1 lemon

2 tbsp chopped fresh parsley, plus extra to garnish

fresh chives to garnish

1 Heat the grill to a moderate heat. Mix together the breadcrumbs, parmesan, lemon zest and chopped parsley.

2 Lay the open mussels on a baking tray and sprinkle with the lemon juice. Spoon a little of the breadcrumb mixture over each open mussel.

3 Put the baking tray under the grill and cook for 5 minutes until the mussels are cooked and the breadcrumb topping is beginning to brown.

Serve garnished with the extra parsley and fresh chives.

Tip Green-lipped mussels are a large variety of mussel that comes from New Zealand. They are available already opened so that you get just one half of the shells with the mussel meat attached.

scallops with tomato & orange sauce

20 mins

serves 4

450g (1lb) large scallops
225g (8oz) tomatoes
juice of 2 oranges
100ml (3½fl oz) fish stock
4 tbsp dry white wine
2 tsp white wine vinegar
½ tsp caster sugar
black pepper
3 tbsp olive oil
few fresh basil leaves for garnish

1 Put the tomatoes in a glass bowl and cover with boiling water for 30 seconds. Drain, peel and chop them.
2 Place the tomatoes in a blender or food processor with the orange juice, stock, wine, vinegar, sugar and black pepper. Blitz until smooth.
3 Strain the mixture into a saucepan and bring it to the boil. Simmer for 5 minutes until reduced by half. Whisk in 1 tbsp oil to make the sauce smooth and glossy.
4 Meanwhile prepare the scallops for frying. Heat 2 tbsp oil in a frying-pan. When the oil is very hot add the scallops and sear them for 2 minutes, turning them over and cooking for 30 seconds more. Remove from the pan and let them rest for 1 minute.
5 Pour the sauce on to 4 soup plates and divide the scallops between them.
Serve garnished with fresh basil leaves and with crusty white bread.

new potato & spinach frittata

30 mins

serves 4

500g (1lb 2oz) cooked new potatoes, sliced

150g (5½oz) baby spinach leaves, washed

1 tbsp olive oil

150g (5½oz) red onions, finely chopped

1 red pepper, chopped

1 garlic clove, crushed

6 spring onions, chopped

3 eggs

4 tbsp milk

1 tbsp each finely chopped fresh basil, chives and parsley

salt and pepper

25g (1oz) parmesan, grated

25g (1oz) cheddar, grated

green salad to serve

1 Heat the oil in a large frying-pan with a flameproof handle and sauté the onions and pepper for 5 minutes until softened.

2 Add the spinach, garlic and spring onions and continue to fry for 2 minutes or until the spinach has wilted. Stir in the potato slices.

3 Beat the eggs in a large bowl with the milk and herbs. Season to taste. Pour the mixture over the vegetables, reduce the heat and cook for 10-12 minutes until the egg begins to set.

4 Meanwhile, heat the grill to medium. Sprinkle the cheeses over the frittata then place the pan under the grill for 2 minutes or until the cheese has melted and turned golden. **Serve** the frittata, cut in wedges, with a green salad.

asparagus benedict

30 mins

serves 4

4 eggs

650g (1lb 7oz) asparagus tips

85g (3oz) butter

2 egg yolks

1 tsp white wine vinegar

salt and finely ground white pepper

1 Bring a large pan of water to the boil. Add the asparagus and cook for about 5 minutes.
2 Meanwhile, poach the 4 eggs in a little simmering water for about 4 minutes.
3 To start making the hollandaise sauce, melt the butter in a small pan until it is clear and bubbling, then remove from the heat.
4 Place the egg yolks in a blender with the white wine vinegar and blitz. Keep the blades whizzing and add the hot melted butter in a steady trickle to form a smooth sauce. Season with salt and pepper.
5 Drain the asparagus, then lift the eggs out of the water with a slotted spoon. Arrange some asparagus and a poached egg on each plate.
Serve the hollandaise sauce drizzled over the asparagus and eggs.

 Tip The hollandaise sauce must be made in a blender or with a hand blender. Such a small quantity of ingredients would get lost rather than blended in a food processor bowl.

20 mins

fried tomatoes & poached eggs

serves 4

4 beefsteak tomatoes

4 eggs

55g (2oz) polenta

2 tbsp olive oil

4 slices onion bread

freshly ground black pepper, to serve

watercress, to serve

1 Place the polenta in a dry frying-pan over high heat and toast for 3-5 minutes.
2 Cut the tomatoes in slices and coat with the toasted polenta.
3 Heat the oil in a frying-pan over moderate heat and fry the coated tomatoes for 3 minutes, each side, until crisp. Drain on kitchen paper.
4 Meanwhile, heat the grill to high and toast the bread. Pour some water into a clean frying-pan – to a depth of about 5cm (2in) – and bring to the boil.
5 Crack the eggs, one by one, into a saucer and slip into the water. Turn off the heat and cover the pan. Leave to poach for 3 minutes until the whites are set and the yolks runny.
6 Meanwhile, arrange the toast on individual plates and top with the tomatoes. Drain the eggs and place on top of the tomatoes.
Serve sprinkled with freshly ground black pepper and garnished with the watercress.

30 mins

goat's cheese & cheddar pâté

serves 8

225g (8oz) soft goat's cheese

225g (8oz) mature cheddar cheese, finely grated

1 garlic clove, crushed

6 tbsp chopped fresh chives

black pepper

3 tbsp milk

chive flowers, snipped (optional)

lamb's lettuce to garnish

1 Soften the goat's cheese in a bowl using a wooden spoon. Add the cheddar and garlic and 1 tbsp chives. Season with black pepper and mix to a thick paste. Use a little milk if necessary to loosen the mix.

2 Transfer the paste to a work surface and roll into a sausage shape approximately 4cm (1½in) in diameter.

3 Roll the sausage in the remaining chives – and the chive flowers if using. Wrap in greaseproof paper and chill in the fridge for 15 minutes. Cut the pâté into slices. Garnish with lamb's lettuce.

Serve the pâté with small pieces of warm crisp toast.

Tip Use cream cheese as an alternative to the goat's cheese and replace the cheddar with your favourite hard cheese if you wish.

25 mins

leek & feta vol-au-vent

serves 4

375g (13oz) packet puff pastry

115g (4oz) leeks, sliced

125g (4½oz) feta cheese, crumbled

2 tbsp pesto

25g (1oz) butter

salt and pepper

8 cherry tomatoes, quartered

2 tbsp pinenuts

1 egg, beaten

1 Pre-heat the oven to 200°C/400°F/gas 6. Roll out the pastry and cut out 4 saucer-size circles. Mark a line round the circles, about 1cm (½in) in from the edge. Spread the pesto over the centre circles, place on a baking tray and chill.

2 Melt the butter in a frying-pan and sweat the leeks until soft, then season. Spread evenly over the pastry circle and top with the cheese, tomatoes and pinenuts.

3 Brush the edges of the pastry with the beaten egg and place near the top of the oven. Bake for 12-15 minutes until the pastry has risen and is golden and the cheese begins to melt.

Serve with a herb salad.

Tip Sliced goat's cheese, grated gruyère or sliced mozzarella can be used instead of the feta.

30 mins

mixed vegetable & cheese balls

serves 8

2 red peppers, trimmed, halved and deseeded

4 celery sticks, finely chopped

small bunch spring onions, chopped

2 tbsp chopped fresh parsley

55g (2oz) pinenuts

115g (4oz) parmesan, finely grated

115g (4oz) fresh breadcrumbs

2 tbsp olive oil

1 egg, beaten

salt and pepper

16 basil leaves

1 Pre-heat the grill to high. Lay the peppers, skin side up, on a baking sheet and place under the grill. Leave for 5-6 minutes until the skin starts to blacken. Remove and place in a plastic bag, then seal.

2 Pre-heat the oven to 200°C/400°F/gas 6. Mix the breadcrumbs, parmesan, olive oil and egg together until you have a sticky mixture. Add the celery, spring onion, parsley and pinenuts and seasoning.

3 Peel skins off the peppers. Cut half the peppers into strips and half into dice. Add the diced peppers to the mix.

4 Shape the mixture into 16 balls and wrap a pepper strip round each one. Secure with a cocktail stick. Thread a basil leaf on each stick, then put the balls on a lightly oiled baking sheet and bake for 15 minutes.

Serve the vegetable balls drizzled with a little olive oil.

three-cheese pitta pizza

20 mins

serves 4

115g (4oz) ready-grated mozzarella

115g (4oz) mature cheddar, grated

115g (4oz) taleggio cheese, thinly sliced

4 pitta breads

1 tbsp vegetable oil

6 tbsp tomato ketchup

1 tsp Tabasco sauce

2 red onions, chopped

4 tomatoes, sliced

1 large red pepper, chopped

2 garlic cloves, crushed

2 tbsp olive oil

4 black olives

55g (2oz) parmesan cheese, grated

basil leaves and marjoram leaves to garnish

1 Pre-heat the oven to 190°C/375°F/gas 5.

2 Brush the vegetable oil over a baking sheet and arrange the pittas on it.

3 Mix the ketchup with the Tabasco sauce. Spread some on each pitta. Sprinkle cheddar and mozzarella evenly on top. Divide the onions, tomatoes and pepper between the breads and top with taleggio.

4 Mix the garlic and olive oil together and then drizzle over the pizzas. Place an olive in the centre of each pizza. Bake in the oven for 10 minutes until the cheese has melted.

Serve straight from the oven, sprinkled with parmesan and fresh herbs.

sweetcorn chowder in a crusty roll

25 mins

serves 4

4 large crusty bread rolls

2 tbsp olive oil

1 onion, finely chopped

1 potato, finely diced

600ml (21fl oz) semi-skimmed milk

150ml (5fl oz) vegetable stock

salt and pepper

200g (7oz) frozen sweetcorn, thawed

150ml (5fl oz) single cream

pinch turmeric

1 tsp cornflour

ground paprika

1 Pre-heat the oven to 200°C/400°F/gas 6.

2 Cut off the top of each bread roll and remove the soft bread from the centre. Place the lid back on the top and bake for 20 minutes.

3 Heat the oil in a medium pan and add the onion and potato. Fry for 5 minutes.

4 Add the milk and stock, season, bring to the boil and simmer for 10 minutes. Then stir in the sweetcorn, cream and turmeric.

5 Mix the cornflour with a little water to form a paste. Bring the soup to the boil and stir in the cornflour paste. Simmer for 1 minute to thicken.

Serve by ladling the soup into each bread roll. Sprinkle ground paprika over the soup.

Tip Thaw sweetcorn by placing it in a sieve and pouring boiling water over it.

15 mins

fried mushroom roll with smoked cheese

serves 4

2 large ciabatta rolls

4 large field mushrooms, wiped

150g (5½oz) smoked mozzarella, sliced

115g (4oz) soft butter

1 tbsp grainy Dijon mustard

4 tbsp extra virgin olive oil

2 garlic cloves, peeled

2 tsp chopped fresh oregano

pepper

fresh oregano leaves to garnish

1 Pre-heat the oven to 220°C/425°F/gas 7. Slice each roll in half and spread both sides with a little butter and mustard. Bake in the oven for 5 minutes.

2 Heat the oil in a frying-pan and fry the garlic until soft.

3 Discard the garlic, increase the heat and fry the mushrooms for 2 minutes on each side until they start to release their juices.

4 Remove the rolls from the oven, top each one with a mushroom, then drizzle the juices over. Divide the cheese between the rolls and sprinkle with a little chopped oregano. Season with pepper, then return to the oven and cook for 5 minutes until the cheese is melted.

Serve the mushroom rolls with fresh oregano leaves sprinkled on top.

30 mins

vegetarian pitta parcels

serves 4

4 pitta breads, cut in half widthways

1 small aubergine, diced

3 tbsp olive oil

salt and pepper

125g (4½oz) couscous

4 tomatoes, skinned, deseeded and roughly chopped

55g (2oz) raisins

55g (2oz) almonds, chopped and toasted

3 tbsp chopped fresh coriander

zest and juice of 1 lemon

1 Pre-heat the oven to 180°C/350°F/gas 4. Place the aubergine in a roasting tin and pour on 1 tbsp oil. Season and mix thoroughly to coat. Roast for 12-15 minutes or until golden brown.

2 Pour 225ml (8fl oz) boiling water on to the couscous and set aside for 5 minutes. Fork through the couscous and combine with the aubergine, tomatoes, raisins, almonds, coriander, lemon zest and juice, and the remaining oil; season to taste.

3 Divide the couscous mixture between the pittas; place on a baking sheet and bake for 5 minutes.

Serve with a green salad.

25 mins

roasted vegetables on toasted focaccia

serves 4

8 long slices focaccia bread

1 red pepper, halved

1 yellow pepper, halved

4 tbsp olive oil

1 courgette, sliced

1 aubergine, sliced

1 red onion

1 artichoke heart

3 small leeks, split

6 large mushrooms

1 garlic clove, peeled

fresh parmesan shavings

1 tbsp fresh parsley leaves

½ tbsp cracked black peppercorns

salt and pepper

1 Pre-heat the grill to high. Rub the peppers with olive oil. Grill until the skins blacken. Cool, peel the skins off then slice the peppers into 8.

2 Drizzle 2 tbsp olive oil over the courgettes and aubergines. Cut the onion and artichoke into 8 pieces. Bring a small pan of water to the boil and blanch the onion and leeks in the boiling water for 2 minutes.

3 Pre-heat the grill to high again. Refresh the onion and leeks under cold water. Brush all the vegetables and mushrooms with olive oil and season. Toast the slices of focaccia on both sides. Grill the mushrooms for 5 minutes and the vegetables for 2 minutes.

4 Rub the toasted bread with garlic and brush with olive oil. Pile the vegetables on top.

Serve with parmesan, parsley and peppercorns.

roasted vegetable tartlets

25 mins

serves 4

225g (8oz) ready-made shortcrust pastry

1 red onion, roughly chopped

1 courgette, roughly chopped

1 yellow pepper, deseeded and roughly chopped

2 baby aubergines, roughly chopped

75g (2¾oz) cherry tomatoes, halved

2 tbsp olive oil

salt and black pepper

25g (1oz) pitted black olives, quartered

2 tbsp pesto

25g (1oz) gruyère, grated

1 Pre-heat the oven to 200°C/400°F/gas 6. Roll out the pastry and use to line four 7.5cm (3in) loose-bottomed flan tins; set aside to chill for a few minutes.

2 Put the vegetables and tomatoes into a roasting tin and mix with the oil until well coated; season to taste.

3 Bake the pastry cases blind for 20 minutes and at the same time, roast the vegetables for 20 minutes until golden in colour.

4 Add the olives and pesto to the roasted vegetables and mix thoroughly. Divide the mixture between the pastry cases and top with the gruyère cheese.

5 Return to the oven for 5 minutes until the cheese is melted and golden.

Serve hot or cold, with a leafy salad.

20 mins

aubergine with a tomato sauce

serves 4

2 large aubergines, cut into thick slices

2 tbsp olive oil

2 tsp cumin seeds

100g (3½oz) canned chopped tomatoes

100g (3½oz) natural yoghurt

salt and black pepper

fresh coriander leaves, to garnish

1 Put a ridged griddle pan over moderate to high heat. Lightly brush the aubergine slices with the oil and griddle for 3-4 minutes until the flesh is soft. Alternatively, cook them under a hot grill. Set aside.

2 Meanwhile, heat a small frying-pan over high heat and dry-fry the cumin seeds for a few seconds until they begin to colour. Remove from the pan and set aside. When cool, grind them to a powder in a spice mill or using a pestle and mortar.

3 Put the tomatoes in a saucepan and cook for 10 minutes, stirring occasionally, until they have reduced and thickened. Set aside to cool.

4 Stir the ground cumin and yoghurt into the cooled tomato sauce; season to taste.

Serve the aubergine slices with the tomato and yoghurt sauce and garnished with the fresh coriander leaves.

potato & horseradish rösti

20 mins

serves 4

4 potatoes, peeled

1 tbsp creamed horseradish

1 beaten egg

6 spring onions, finely chopped

salt and freshly ground black pepper

2 tbsp sunflower oil

4 tbsp crème fraîche and 1 tbsp chopped fresh parsley, to serve

1 Grate the potatoes and, using your hands, squeeze out any excess moisture. Put the potato in a bowl and add the egg, horseradish, spring onions and season to taste. Mix together well.

2 Heat the oil in a large frying-pan. Drop 8 mounds of the potato mixture into the pan and then press down with a spatula until the rösti are about 5mm (¼in) thick. (Cook your rösti in batches if your frying-pan isn't big enough.)

3 Fry over medium heat for 3-5 minutes on each side until they are firm and golden. Drain on kitchen paper.

Serve two rösti per person, each topped with 1 tbsp crème fraîche and garnished with the chopped parsley.

30 mins

brie & roasted tomato rösti

serves 4

175g (6oz) brie, cut into chunks

15-20 baby plum tomatoes, cut in half

5 tbsp olive oil

1 tbsp chopped fresh oregano

salt and freshly ground black pepper

4 potatoes, peeled

1-2 tbsp double cream

sprigs of fresh sage and oregano, to garnish

1 Pre-heat the oven to 220°C/425°F/gas 7 and put a large pan of salted water on to boil. Put the tomatoes in a roasting tin and mix with 3 tbsp oil and the chopped oregano; season to taste. Roast for 15-20 minutes until the tomatoes have softened.

2 Meanwhile, boil the potatoes for 10 minutes; drain and return to the pan. Break up the potatoes roughly with a wooden spoon. Mix in enough double cream to bind the potatoes together; season to taste.

3 Heat the remaining oil in a frying-pan. Add the potato and press into a large flat round with a spatula. Cook over moderate heat for 3-5 minutes on each side until well browned. Cut into 4 wedges. **Serve** immediately topped with chunks of brie; the warmth of the potato will melt the cheese slightly. Add the roasted tomatoes and garnish with the sage and oregano.

pasta, rice, noodles and polenta

25 mins

chicken, broccoli & pasta gratin

serves 4

350g (12oz) skinned, boned cooked chicken

225g (8oz) broccoli florets

175g (6oz) fusilli

2 sticks celery, thinly sliced

300ml (10fl oz) passata

25g (1oz) fresh white breadcrumbs

¼ tsp dried herbes de Provence

1 Bring a large pan of salted water to the boil and cook the fusilli according to the packet instructions. Drain.

2 Meanwhile, bring another pan of salted water to the boil. Add the broccoli and celery and cook for about 5 minutes, until the broccoli starts to soften. Drain the vegetables in a colander, and quickly refresh them under a cold tap. Set aside.

3 Heat the grill to high. Pour the passata into a saucepan and gently warm it up until it comes to a simmer.

4 Trim any fat off the chicken, and cut it into bite sized pieces. Add them to the passata with the broccoli, celery and pasta, and simmer for 5 minutes.

5 Pour the mixture into a shallow flameproof gratin dish. Scatter breadcrumbs and herbs evenly over the top, and grill until the sauce is bubbling and the topping is golden.

Serve hot with crusty bread.

25 mins

chicken & mascarpone pasta

serves 4

4 chicken breasts, boned

250g (9oz) mascarpone cheese

350g (12oz) penne

1 tbsp olive oil

salt and pepper

12 marinated red pepper strips (see Tip below)

125g (4½oz) bag of rocket leaves

1 Heat the grill to medium. Rub the olive oil into the chicken breasts, then season.
2 Grill the breasts for about 15 minutes, turning once, until the juices run clear when they are pierced with a fine skewer.
3 Meanwhile, cook the penne. Drain it and reserve a little of the cooking water, then return the pasta to the pan.
4 Mix the mascarpone cheese, red pepper strips and rocket leaves into the pasta. Heat it very gently while stirring.
5 Loosen the pasta with some of the cooking water, then season to taste.
Serve the grilled chicken, sliced into wide strips, on top of the pasta salad.

Tip You can buy marinated red peppers in jars from delicatessens or large supermarkets. If you can't find them, grill red peppers until their skins blister, then peel and slice into strips.

rich lamb pasta bake

30 mins

serves 4

450g (1lb) lean minced lamb

225g (8oz) pasta shapes

1 onion, finely chopped

2 garlic cloves, crushed

440g (15oz) jar ragù sauce with basil

2 eggs

142ml (5fl oz) pot soured cream

85g (3oz) cheddar cheese, grated

sprigs of basil, to serve

1 Pre-heat oven to 200°C/400°F/gas 6.

2 Bring a large pan of salted water to the boil and cook the pasta according to the instructions on the packet. Drain when *al dente*.

3 Heat a large frying-pan and dry-fry the lamb with the onions and garlic over a moderate heat for 10 minutes.

4 Drain or spoon any surplus fat from the mince, then stir in the ragù and the pasta. Pour the mixture into an ovenproof gratin dish.

5 Beat the eggs, then the soured cream and the cheddar cheese together. Season well and pour over the lamb mixture.

6 Bake for 15 minutes until golden and bubbling.

Serve garnished with sprigs of fresh basil.

30 mins

pasta & meatballs in spicy tomato sauce

serves 4

500g (1lb 2oz) pappardelle pasta

500g (1lb 2oz) minced beef

2 x 400g (14oz) cans chopped tomatoes

25g (1oz) fresh breadcrumbs

25g (1oz) bacon, diced

½ onion, grated

4 sprigs oregano, chopped

1 tbsp chopped flatleaf parsley

2 tsp Worcestershire sauce

1 egg, beaten

salt and pepper

3 tbsp olive oil

150ml (5fl oz) red wine

2 dried red chillies, crumbled

dash of Tabasco sauce

1 tbsp tomato purée

55g (2oz) green olives, pitted

fresh oregano to garnish

1 Mix the breadcrumbs, bacon, onion, oregano, parsley, Worcestershire sauce and egg with the mince. Season, then shape into 16 small balls.
2 Heat 2 tbsp olive oil in a frying-pan and brown the meatballs for 5 minutes. Add the wine and simmer for 2 minutes until reduced.
3 Drop the pasta into a large pan of lightly salted boiling water and cook until tender.
4 Add tomatoes, chillies, Tabasco and tomato purée to the meatballs. Simmer for 15 minutes. Stir in the olives.
5 Drain pasta and toss in the olive oil and meatball sauce.
Serve with fresh oregano.

20 mins

pasta spirals with salami & tomato

serves 4

500g (1lb 2oz) pasta spirals

85g (3oz) salami, thinly sliced and cut into strips

400g (14oz) can chopped tomatoes

4 tbsp olive oil

2 red onions, finely chopped

1 large garlic clove, finely chopped

1 tbsp tomato purée

200ml (7fl oz) chicken or vegetable stock

salt and pepper

55g (2oz) coarse ciabatta or focaccia breadcrumbs

fresh parmesan shavings to garnish

mixed salad leaves to serve

1 Bring a large pan of salted water to the boil, add the pasta spirals and cook until tender.

2 Heat 2 tbsp olive oil in a frying-pan, add the onion and fry for 5 minutes. Add the garlic and salami and fry for a further 2 minutes.

3 Add the chopped tomatoes, tomato purée and stock to the frying-pan and simmer for 10 minutes. Taste and season.

4 Heat the remaining oil in a frying-pan and fry the breadcrumbs for 2-3 minutes until golden, then scatter over the sauce.

Serve the pasta tossed in the salami and tomato sauce, with parmesan shavings on top. Serve a mixed green salad on the side.

herby sausage & garlic penne

25 mins

serves 4

450g (1lb) pork and herb sausages

280g (10oz) penne pasta

salt and pepper

4 tbsp olive oil

1 garlic clove, crushed

2 shallots, chopped

6 gherkins, chopped

1 small bunch flatleaf parsley, chopped, saving a few whole leaves for a garnish

1 Pre-heat the grill to high. Grill the sausages for 12-15 minutes turning occasionally until browned all over. Slice diagonally into bite-sized pieces and set aside.

2 Meanwhile bring a large pan of salted water to the boil. Cook the pasta according to the packet instructions.

3 When the pasta is cooked, drain and refresh briefly under cold water, then toss in half the olive oil.

4 Heat the rest of the oil in a large pan and add the garlic, shallots, gherkins and chopped parsley. Fry for 2-3 minutes.

5 Add the pasta and sausage to the garlic mix. Season, mix well and heat through.

Serve piping hot from the pan, garnished with a few parsley leaves.

Tip Ready-cooked frankfurters are also good with this. Just chop them up and add them to the garlic mix.

chinese chicken with glass noodles

20 mins

serves 4

4 chicken breasts, boned and skinned

225g (8oz) glass noodles

1 tsp sesame oil

2 tbsp vegetable oil

2 tbsp soy sauce

1 tbsp rice vinegar

1 tsp finely chopped ginger

1 tbsp chopped coriander

1 tsp sugar

3-4 spring onions, sliced diagonally

½ small cucumber, cut into julienne strips

coriander leaves to garnish

1 Pre-heat the grill to medium. Coat the breasts in the sesame seed oil and half the soy sauce. Then grill for 10-15 minutes, turning once.

2 Allow the breasts to cool slightly, then slice them thinly crossways and set aside.

3 Cook the glass noodles according to the instructions on the packet. Drain and set them aside.

4 To make a dressing, mix together the vegetable oil, the rest of the soy sauce, vinegar, ginger, coriander and sugar.

5 Put the chicken, noodles, spring onions and cucumber in a salad bowl. Pour the dressing over the top and toss until well mixed.

Serve the salad in individual salad bowls. Garnish each one with coriander leaves.

25 mins

chicken, rice & vegetable stir-fry

serves 4

4 chicken breasts, cut in strips

225g (8oz) rice

2 tbsp vegetable oil

I red onion, sliced

I onion, sliced

2 sticks of celery, sliced

I yellow pepper, chopped

55g (2oz) cooked prawns, chopped

2 pieces stem ginger, sliced

½ tsp cumin seeds

juice of I lemon

4 tbsp soy sauce

pepper

I Bring a large pan of salted water to the boil and add the rice. Cook for 10-12 minutes until just tender. Then drain, rinse under cold running water and drain again.

2 Meanwhile, heat a large frying-pan or wok and add I tbsp oil. When the oil is smoking, add the chicken strips and stir-fry over a high heat until golden brown. Remove from the pan with a slotted spoon and keep on one side.

3 Heat the rest of the oil in the hot pan, add the onions, celery and pepper and stir-fry for 5 minutes until slightly softened. Add the prawns.

4 Return the chicken to the pan and stir in the rice, stem ginger, cumin seeds, lemon juice and soy sauce. Stir-fry until the rice and prawns are hot. Season to taste with pepper.

Serve the stir-fry in individual bowls, with more soy sauce on the side.

25 mins

chicken with gorgonzola polenta

serves 4

500g (1lb 2oz) granulated polenta

4 chicken breasts

115g (4oz) gorgonzola

25g (1oz) butter

salt and pepper

bunch of fresh sage leaves

green salad to serve

1 Pre-heat the grill to high. Make up the polenta mash following the packet instructions. Crumble half of the gorgonzola into the polenta and season well.

2 Melt the butter in a frying-pan and fry the chicken breasts for 8 minutes on either side until cooked through. Season well with salt and pepper.

3 Crumble the remaining gorgonzola over the chicken breasts and place under the grill. Grill for 2-3 minutes until the cheese starts to melt.

4 Spoon a mound of polenta on to each plate and place a chicken breast on top. **Serve** garnished with sage leaves, with a green salad on the side.

Tip Replace the gorgonzola with the same amount of dolcelatte if you wish.

30 mins

open lasagne of smoked haddock & wild mushrooms

serves 4

8 sheets fresh lasagne

450g (1lb) undyed smoked haddock, skinned and cut into 5cm (2in) chunks

25g (1oz) butter

375g (12oz) leeks, trimmed and finely sliced

115g (4oz) wild mushrooms, washed and cut in half

250g (9oz) mascarpone

150ml (5fl oz) fish stock

chopped fresh chives

1 In a large frying-pan, cook the leeks in butter for 5 minutes. Add the mushrooms and cook for 3 minutes.

2 Mix in the mascarpone and fish stock, then add the fish pieces. Poach for 5 minutes until cooked evenly.

3 Put lasagne sheets in a pan of boiling salted water and cook for 3-4 minutes. Drain, separate the sheets and keep them warm in hot water.

4 To assemble the open lasagne, lay one sheet of pasta on each plate. Top each with 2-3 tbsp fish mixture saving some of the liquor to pour over the lasagne. Cover with a second sheet of lasagne and spoon over a little of the reserved liquor.

Serve immediately with a sprinkling of chopped chives and pepper.

15 mins

gorgonzola & prawn pasta

serves 4

175g (6oz) gorgonzola, chopped

200g (7oz) raw, peeled king prawns

350g (12oz) fettuccine

1 tbsp oil

225g (8oz) leeks, sliced

115g (4oz) crème fraîche

salt and pepper

1 tbsp chopped fresh chives

crusty bread to serve

1 Bring a large pan of salted water to the boil and add the pasta. Cook following the packet instructions.
2 Heat the oil in a frying-pan and sweat the leeks gently for 5-6 minutes.
3 Add the prawns to the frying-pan and cook for 4 minutes. Add the crème fraîche and gorgonzola. Season to taste but be careful with the salt as gorgonzola is already very salty. Keep stirring until the cheese melts.
4 Drain the pasta and toss with the sauce. Sprinkle with chives.
Serve with crusty bread.

Tip When melting gorgonzola into a sauce, it is best to buy a cheese which is more creamy than blue. This improves the appearance of the finished sauce.

20 mins

penne with ginger, crab & asparagus

serves 4

500g (1lb 2oz) penne

2.5cm (1in) piece of root ginger, peeled and grated

350g (12oz) white crabmeat

200g (7oz) asparagus spears

4 tbsp double cream

grated zest of 1 lemon

juice of ½ lemon

salt and pepper

2.5cm (1in) finely shredded root ginger to garnish

1 Cook the pasta in a large pan of boiling lightly salted water for 10-12 minutes.

2 Meanwhile, blanch the asparagus in a small pan of boiling salted water for 1 minute. Drain and refresh in cold water.

3 Heat the cream in a small saucepan. Add the ginger, lemon zest and juice. Stir in the crab and the asparagus spears and heat through. Season well.

4 Drain the pasta and toss with the crab sauce.

Serve with a garnish of shredded ginger shallow-fried until golden brown.

Tip Fresh crabmeat gives the best flavour for this dish but if you have trouble finding this, use two cans of white crabmeat instead.

mussels in dill sauce with tagliatelle

30 mins

serves 4

2kg (4½lb) live mussels, cleaned

300ml (10fl oz) dry white wine

2 bay leaves

2 sprigs fresh flatleaf parsley

2 slices of lemon

salt and black pepper

1 tbsp cornflour

10-12 strands saffron (optional)

3 tbsp chopped fresh dill

400g (14oz) fresh tagliatelle

250g (9oz) fromage frais

1 Put the mussels in a very large saucepan. Add wine, bay leaves, parsley and lemon. Cover and cook over a high heat for 6-8 minutes, shaking frequently, until all the mussels have opened. Discard any that don't.

2 Drain the mussels, saving the cooking liquor in a saucepan. When cool enough to handle, remove the mussels from their shells and put in a bowl.

3 Bring the cooking liquor to the boil and boil until reduced to 300ml (10fl oz). Mix the cornflour with 1 tbsp cold water and stir into the reduced liquor.

4 Add the saffron, if using, and return to the boil, stirring continuously. Reduce the heat, add 2 tbsp dill and simmer for 5 minutes.

5 Meanwhile, cook the tagliatelle in a large pan of salted water, according to the packet instructions.

6 Gradually whisk the fromage frais into the sauce and add the mussels; heat through. Drain the pasta and stir into the sauce.

Serve sprinkled with pepper and the remaining dill.

20 mins

scallop & roast pepper pasta

serves 4

450g (1lb) large scallops

2 red peppers, quartered

2 yellow peppers, quartered

400g (14oz) spaghetti

½ tsp flaked dried chillies

zest and juice of 1 lemon

4 tbsp olive oil

6 tbsp finely chopped fresh parsley

salt and pepper

3 garlic cloves, crushed

1 lemon, cut into 8 wedges

grated parmesan cheese to serve

1 Pre-heat the grill to high. Cook the spaghetti according to packet instructions. Drain and refresh.

2 Arrange the peppers, skin side up, on the grill pan. Grill for 6 minutes until their skins blacken. Transfer to a bowl and cover with plastic wrap.

3 Peel and dice the peppers when cool. Return them to the bowl and mix with the chilli, lemon zest and 2 tbsp oil. Stir in half the parsley.

4 Clean and prepare scallops for cooking. Toss the scallops in 1 tbsp oil and season. Heat a large frying-pan and sear the scallops for 2-3 minutes, turning once.

5 Heat the remaining oil in a frying-pan. Fry garlic for 1 minute and stir in the roast pepper mixture. Once warm, add the scallops, lemon juice and spaghetti. Toss and season with pepper and parsley.

Serve the pasta with lemon wedges and grated parmesan.

squid & prawn risotto

30 mins

serves 4

225g (8oz) risotto rice

115g (4oz) fresh squid, cleaned and sliced into rings

115g (4oz) king prawns, heads removed

4 baby squid to garnish

850ml (30fl oz) fish stock

10 strands of saffron

4 tbsp vegetable oil

bunch of spring onions, chopped

2 garlic cloves, crushed

115g (4oz) sugar snap peas

85g (3oz) frozen peas, thawed

salt and pepper

1 tsp fresh chopped mint

1 tbsp chilli oil

sprigs fresh mint and oregano

1 Heat fish stock in a pan and add saffron strands to infuse.
2 Heat half the oil in a large pan, add the garlic and spring onions and cook for 5 minutes until softened. Add the rice and cook for 1 minute, stirring all the time, until transparent.
3 Add the stock to the rice, a ladle at a time. Stir until it is absorbed. Repeat until three-quarters of the stock is used up.
4 Heat the remaining oil in a frying-pan. Stir-fry the squid, prawns and baby squid for 2-3 minutes, then set aside.
5 Add sugar snaps and peas to the rice with rest of the stock and cook until tender. Season and stir in the mint and chilli oil. After picking out the baby squid, mix the remaining seafood mixture into the rice.
Serve garnished with baby squid, mint and oregano sprigs.

spicy seafood jambalaya

30 mins

serves 4

450g (1lb) seafood mix
1 tbsp olive oil
1 tsp pimentón
3 garlic cloves, crushed
1 tsp chilli flakes
1 onion, roughly chopped
1 green pepper, diced
1 large courgette, diced
150g (5½oz) chorizo sausage, thinly sliced
1 tsp oregano
350g (12oz) long-grain rice
700ml (25fl oz) fish stock
3 tbsp flatleaf parsley
flatleaf parsley, to garnish
fried onions, to garnish

1 Heat the olive oil in a large saucepan. Add the pimentón, garlic, chilli flakes and onion. Cook for 2 minutes.
2 Add the pepper, courgette, chorizo sausage and oregano to the saucepan and gently fry for about 3 minutes.
3 Add the rice and fry for 2 minutes. Pour in the fish stock and bring to the boil, then simmer for 15 minutes, stirring occasionally, until the liquid has been absorbed.
4 Stir in the seafood mix and cook for about 5 minutes until completely heated through. Mix in the flatleaf parsley.
Serve garnished with flatleaf parsley and fried onions.

Tip Pimentón is Spanish paprika with a distinctive smoky taste. If you can't find it, use paprika instead.

25 mins

stir-fried asparagus & crab

serves 4

350g (12oz) thin asparagus, trimmed and cut into 5cm (2in) lengths

250g (9oz) fresh white crabmeat

115g (4oz) rice noodles

2 tbsp peanut oil

1 bunch spring onions, sliced and separated into white and green pieces

2.5cm (1in) fresh root ginger, peeled and cut into thin strips

115g (4oz) cooked samphire

2 tbsp oyster sauce

4 tbsp vegetable or chicken stock

1 tbsp sesame oil

salt and pepper

1 tbsp toasted sesame seeds

1 Place the rice noodles in a bowl and cover with boiling water and leave to soak.
2 Heat the peanut oil in a wok or large frying-pan until hot. Add the ginger and white pieces of spring onion and stir-fry for 3 minutes. Then add the asparagus and the samphire and stir-fry for a further 3 minutes.
3 Add the oyster sauce and stock, cover and cook for 2-3 minutes. Uncover and add the crab and the rest of the spring onions. Cook for 2 minutes stirring gently to avoid breaking up the crab.
4 Drain the noodles, add them to the wok with the sesame oil and season. Toss to mix.
Serve in individual bowls, sprinkled with sesame seeds.

20 mins

tortellini & tomato balsamic sauce

serves 4

500g (1lb 2oz) ready-made spinach-stuffed tortellini

25g (1oz) sun-dried tomatoes in oil, drained and roughly chopped

2 tbsp balsamic vinegar

3 tbsp olive oil

2 garlic cloves, sliced

700g jar passata

3-4 tbsp sun-dried tomato paste

7 tbsp mascarpone

1 small bunch fresh basil, finely sliced

1 Drop the tortellini into a large pan of boiling salted water and cook according to packet instructions.

2 Heat 2 tbsp oil in a large frying-pan and add the garlic. Fry for 1 minute. Add the vinegar and simmer until it has almost evaporated.

3 Pour in the passata and sun-dried tomato paste. Simmer gently for 10 minutes.

4 Stir 3 tbsp of mascarpone, the basil and most of the sun-dried tomatoes into the sauce.

5 Drain the tortellini and toss in the remaining olive oil. Coat the pasta well with the sauce.

Serve the sauce and pasta with 1 tbsp of mascarpone per portion. Scatter the remaining sun-dried tomatoes on top.

Tip **Reserve the oil from the sun-dried tomatoes. It makes an excellent salad dressing.**

20 mins

red pepper & broccoli pasta

serves 4

1 red pepper, deseeded and thinly sliced

280g (10oz) broccoli florets

400g (14oz) fusilli

2-3 tbsp olive oil

2 garlic cloves, crushed

1 red onion, halved and thinly sliced

2 tbsp red pesto

55g (2oz) pinenuts, lightly toasted under the grill

salt and pepper

freshly grated parmesan, to serve

1 Bring a large pan of salted water to the boil. Add the pasta and cook for 10-12 minutes or according to packet instructions; drain.

2 Meanwhile, heat 1 tbsp olive oil in a frying-pan and fry the garlic and onion gently for 2-3 minutes until softened but not browned. Add the red pepper and continue frying for 2-3 minutes, stirring regularly.

3 Blanch the broccoli in boiling water until just tender, then drain.

4 Thin the red pesto with 1 tbsp olive oil and toss with the pasta, broccoli, onion, garlic, pepper and pinenuts in a large saucepan. Season to taste. Add another tablespoon or so of olive oil to moisten the dish if you like.

Serve as soon as the mixture is hot, with a large bowl of parmesan for sprinkling over the top.

roast vegetable penne

30 mins

serves 4

1 small aubergine, cut into chunks

1 red pepper, deseeded and roughly chopped

1 red onion, roughly chopped

1 large courgette, sliced

salt and pepper

2 tbsp olive oil

350g (12oz) penne

25g (1oz) butter

1 garlic clove, crushed

55g (2oz) fresh breadcrumbs

1 Pre-heat the oven to 200°C/400°F/gas 6. Put the vegetables in a roasting tin and season to taste. Drizzle on the oil and toss everything together. Roast for 25 minutes until softened and golden.

2 Meanwhile, bring a large saucepan of water to the boil and cook the pasta for 10 minutes or according to packet instructions; drain.

3 Melt the butter in a frying-pan and gently fry the garlic for 30 seconds, without letting it brown. Add the breadcrumbs and fry for a couple more minutes until golden.

4 Mix the roast vegetables with the drained pasta.

Serve sprinkled with the fried garlic and breadcrumbs.

Tip Why not try mixing some grated parmesan in with the breadcrumbs for a cheesy topping?

30 mins

pappardelle with aubergine sauce

serves 4

400g (14oz) fresh pappardelle, or other ribbon pasta

600g (1lb 5oz) baby aubergines, halved lengthways and thinly sliced

1 tbsp olive oil

2 fresh chillies, deseeded and chopped

4 garlic cloves, chopped

1 onion, chopped

1 red pepper, deseeded and chopped

2 tbsp lemon juice

3 tbsp dark soy sauce

225ml (8fl oz) vegetable stock

2 tsp tomato purée

3 tbsp chopped fresh coriander, plus extra to garnish

1 Heat the oil in a frying-pan over high heat and stir-fry the chillies, garlic, onion and red pepper for 3-4 minutes until the onions begin to brown.

2 Add the aubergines and continue frying for 3-4 minutes, stirring frequently.

3 Stir in the lemon juice, soy sauce, stock, tomato purée and season to taste. Simmer for 15 minutes. Raise the heat and boil rapidly for 3-4 minutes until most of the liquid has evaporated. Stir in the chopped coriander.

4 Meanwhile, cook the pasta in boiling salted water for 3-4 minutes or according to packet instructions; drain.

Serve the sauce spooned over the pasta and garnished with the extra coriander.

20 mins

mushroom & sun-dried tomato pasta

serves 4

350g (12oz) penne

450g (1lb) mixed mushrooms, sliced

115g (4oz) sun-dried tomatoes, chopped

4 tbsp olive oil

2 garlic cloves, crushed

2 tsp chopped fresh thyme

225g (8oz) mascarpone

25g (1oz) grated parmesan plus extra for serving

salt and pepper

1 Cook the penne in a large pan of lightly salted boiling water, according to packet instructions. When cooked, drain well.

2 Meanwhile, heat the olive oil in a pan. Add the mushrooms, garlic and thyme and fry gently for 5 minutes.

3 Stir the sun-dried tomatoes, mascarpone and parmesan into the pan and warm through for 5 minutes. Season to taste with salt and pepper.

4 Tip the penne into the pan and toss over a medium heat until hot and well mixed.

Serve with grated parmesan for sprinkling over the top.

Tip You may prefer to use fresh oregano or basil instead of thyme in this dish. As neither are as robust as thyme, add the coarsely chopped leaves to the sauce with the pasta at the end of cooking.

30 mins

sage & garlic beans

serves 4

*400g (14oz) can borlotti
beans, drained*

1 tbsp chopped fresh sage

4 garlic cloves, crushed

5 tbsp olive oil

1 onion, diced

2 carrots, diced

1 celery stick, sliced

600ml (20fl oz) tomato juice

*300ml (10fl oz) vegetable
stock*

115g (4oz) fresh pasta shells

2 tbsp chopped fresh parsley

salt and pepper

*freshly grated parmesan,
to serve*

1 Heat 4 tbsp oil in a large
sauté pan or saucepan and fry
the garlic, onion, carrots,
celery and sage for 5 minutes.
2 Add the tomato juice, stock
and beans. Cover and simmer
gently for 20 minutes.
3 Stir in the fresh pasta and
parsley; season to taste.
Continue to cook for
3-5 minutes or until the pasta
is tender but still *al dente*.
Serve immediately, sprinkled
with the remaining olive oil
and the parmesan.

Tip If you can't get
hold of borlotti
beans, you could
substitute the same
amount of cannellini or
haricot beans.

pasta with spinach & broad beans

30 mins

serves 4

175g (6oz) tortiglioni or rigatoni

350g (12oz) baby spinach leaves, washed and drained

225g (8oz) frozen broad beans, defrosted

2 tbsp olive oil

1 onion, chopped

1 garlic clove, crushed

1 red pepper, sliced

salt and pepper

400g (14oz) can chopped tomatoes

pinch of dried oregano

½ tsp brown sugar

300g (10oz) can artichoke hearts, drained and quartered

55g (2oz) grated parmesan cheese to serve

warm crusty bread to serve

1 Bring a large pan of salted water to the boil. Add the pasta and cook according to the packet instructions; drain.

2 Meanwhile, heat the oil in a saucepan and fry the onion and garlic gently for 5 minutes until softened. Add the red pepper and cook for 2 minutes, then season to taste.

3 Stir the tomatoes, oregano, sugar and black pepper into the pan. Cover and simmer for 10 minutes.

4 Tip the broad beans into the tomato sauce and simmer for 3 minutes. Add the spinach and cook for another 3 minutes.

5 Mix the artichoke hearts and pasta into the sauce as well. Heat through for 1-2 minutes. **Serve** with crusty bread and sprinkled with parmesan.

25 mins

grilled stuffed pasta with tangy cheese

serves 4

300ml ready-made cheese sauce

500g (1lb 2oz) stuffed pasta, such as ravioli

55g (2oz) gruyère, grated

4 tbsp dry white wine

4 plum tomatoes, thickly sliced

115g (4oz) parmesan cheese, grated

55g (2oz) fresh white breadcrumbs

salt and pepper

1 Pre-heat the grill to high. Bring a large pan of water to the boil, drop in the pasta and cook for 10 minutes or according to the packet instructions.

2 Heat the cheese sauce in a saucepan and add the gruyère and white wine. Whisk until the cheese has melted and the white wine is blended in.

3 Drain the pasta and place in an ovenproof dish. Mix the tomato slices with the stuffed pasta. Pour the cheese sauce over. Season generously with black pepper.

4 Sprinkle the parmesan and breadcrumbs over the pasta and tomatoes and place under the hot grill for 5-7 minutes.

Serve the pasta with a green salad and crusty bread.

15 mins

blue cheese & walnut pasta

serves 4

250g (8oz) stilton

175g (6oz) walnut pieces

500g (1lb 2oz) tomato flavoured pappardelle pasta

1 tbsp walnut oil

2 shallots, finely chopped

1 garlic clove, crushed

300ml (10fl oz) double cream

2 tbsp fresh parsley, roughly chopped

salt and pepper

rocket leaves to serve

1 Cook and drain the pasta according to packet instructions.

2 Meanwhile, heat the oil and cook the shallots and garlic until softened.

3 Stir in the walnut pieces and crumble in the stilton. When the cheese starts to melt add the cream and heat until it just begins to boil.

4 Stir the pasta into the sauce, add the parsley and season. **Serve** the pasta in warm bowls with rocket leaves on the side.

Tip You can substitute other blue cheeses, such as Danish blue, gorgonzola, dolcelatte or Roquefort for the stilton.

20 mins

tagliatelle with summer vegetables

serves 4

500g (1lb 2oz) fresh tagliatelle

250g (9oz) thin asparagus

150g (5½oz) green beans

200g (7oz) small courgettes

150g (5½oz) baby leeks

1-2 tbsp olive oil

1 garlic clove, finely chopped

4 tbsp lemon juice

2 tsp chopped fresh tarragon

salt and black pepper

2-3 tbsp chopped fresh flatleaf parsley, to serve

1 Put 2 pans of water on to boil. Trim the asparagus and cut into 2.5cm (1in) lengths. Trim and halve the beans. Thinly slice the courgettes. Trim the leeks, quarter lengthways and cut into 1cm (½in) slices.

2 Put the asparagus and beans into one pan and cook for 4 minutes until just tender. Drain and set aside.

3 Add the pasta to the other pan and cook according to packet instructions.

4 Meanwhile, heat 1 tbsp oil in a large frying-pan and stir-fry the garlic for 30 seconds. Add the courgettes and leeks and stir-fry for 3 minutes or until the courgettes are tender.

5 Add the asparagus and stir-fry for 1 minute, then mix in the lemon juice and tarragon. Remove from the heat and season to taste.

6 Drain the pasta and stir in the cooked vegetables. Moisten with 1 tbsp oil, if necessary.

Serve sprinkled with the parsley and extra black pepper to taste.

20 mins

gnocchi with red pesto & pinenuts

serves 4

500g (1lb 2oz) packet fresh potato gnocchi

250g (9oz) tub mascarpone

200ml (7fl oz) milk

4 tbsp red pesto

4 tbsp pinenuts, toasted

handful of fresh basil leaves

handful of baby spinach

55g (2oz) parmesan cheese, grated, plus extra to serve

1 Bring a large pan of salted water to the boil and add the gnocchi. Boil for 3 minutes or according to packet instructions; drain.

2 Meanwhile, put the mascarpone, milk, red pesto, pinenuts, basil leaves and baby spinach into a saucepan over low heat and stir until the mascarpone melts. Stir in the parmesan cheese.

3 Stir the gnocchi into the mascarpone mixture and continue to heat until the spinach has wilted and the sauce is bubbling.

Serve sprinkled with the extra parmesan.

Tip To toast the pinenuts for this recipe, put them in a frying-pan without any oil over moderate heat and cook for a few minutes until they begin to brown.

30 mins

saffron risotto with vegetables

serves 4

225g (8oz) risotto rice

10-12 strands of saffron

2 garlic cloves, finely sliced

175g (6oz) baby carrots

200g (7oz) leeks, chopped

115g (4oz) asparagus spears, cut into 2cm (¾in) lengths

115g (4oz) green beans, chopped

115g (4oz) frozen peas, thawed

1.2 litres (2 pints) vegetable stock

2 tbsp olive oil

1 tbsp chopped fresh chives

1 tbsp chopped fresh dill

1 tbsp chopped fresh parsley

1 tbsp chopped fresh tarragon

55g (2oz) parmesan, grated

salt and pepper

1 Warm stock in a pan, add saffron and leave to infuse for 10 minutes. Meanwhile, heat oil in a large frying-pan and fry garlic, carrots and leeks for 10 minutes until softened.

2 Bring stock to simmering point. Add rice to vegetables and stir for 1 minute until the grains are glossy.

3 Keep stock simmering. Add a ladle of stock to the rice. Stir until completely absorbed. Continue until there are only 2 ladles of stock left.

4 Add asparagus, beans and peas to rice with rest of stock. Cook for 4-5 minutes until rice and vegetables are tender.

5 Remove the pan from the heat and stir in the herbs, parmesan and seasoning.

Serve with extra parmesan.

25 mins

egyptian rice with green lentils

serves 4

150g (5½oz) easy-cook risotto rice

400g (14oz) can green lentils, drained

salt and pepper

150g (5½oz) macaroni

2 tsp olive oil

150g (5½oz) onions, chopped

2 garlic cloves, crushed

1 tsp cayenne pepper

1 tsp ground coriander

400g (14oz) can chopped tomatoes

2 tbsp chopped fresh parsley

1 Bring a large pan of salted water to the boil. Add the rice and simmer for 5 minutes. Add the macaroni, stir once or twice and cook for another 10 minutes until the rice and pasta are tender. Drain and set aside in a colander.
2 Meanwhile, place the oil and 2 tbsp water in a saucepan. Add the onions and garlic and sauté for 5 minutes until softened. Stir in the spices and cook for 1 minute.
3 Add the tomatoes and lentils to the onions, season to taste and bring the mixture to the boil. Simmer for 10 minutes, stirring occasionally.
4 Mix in the rice and macaroni and add most of the parsley. **Serve** immediately garnished with the rest of the parsley.

Tip If you are not keen on a hot chilli taste, use paprika instead of cayenne.

30 mins

vegetable fried rice with tofu

serves 4

125g (4½oz) easy-cook long-grain rice

115g (4oz) tofu, thinly sliced and cut into strips

55g (2oz) dried mushrooms

3 tbsp sesame oil

1 onion, finely chopped

1 red pepper, chopped

1 carrot, chopped thinly

55g (2oz) frozen peas

2 tbsp soy sauce

2 tbsp lemon juice

chives to garnish

1 Put the mushrooms in a bowl, cover them with boiling water and leave to soak for 20 minutes. Then drain and save the liquid. (If the mushrooms are very large, tear them in half, otherwise leave them whole.)

2 Meanwhile, bring a large pan of salted water to the boil. Add the rice. Boil for 12-15 minutes until tender; drain.

3 When the mushrooms and rice are ready, heat the oil in a large frying-pan or wok. Add the tofu, onions, pepper and carrot and stir-fry briskly for 2-3 minutes.

4 Add the mushrooms and peas and toss around in the pan for another minute.

5 Then tip in the rice and mix well before adding the soy sauce, lemon juice and 1 tbsp of the mushroom soaking liquid. Heat until all the liquid is absorbed, stirring all the time.

Serve garnished with chives, and offer more soy sauce if required.

30 mins

noodles with lentils, spinach & carrots

serves 4

250g (9oz) dried soba noodles

125g (4½oz) Puy lentils

150g (5½oz) fresh spinach leaves, coarsely shredded

75g (2½oz) carrots, finely diced

1 bay leaf

1 tbsp olive oil

3 garlic cloves, chopped

100g (3½oz) red onions, chopped

1 stick celery, finely chopped

2 tsp Dijon mustard

2 tbsp dry sherry

salt and black pepper

2 tbsp chopped fresh parsley

1 Put the lentils and bay leaf into a pan and cover with cold water. Bring to the boil, then simmer for 10-15 minutes until tender; drain.

2 Meanwhile, heat the oil in a saucepan over a very low heat. Add the garlic and onions. Cook, covered, for 7-10 minutes until soft. Put a large pan of water on to boil.

3 Mix the lentils, carrots, celery, mustard and sherry with the onions; season to taste. Raise the heat to medium and cook, covered, for 2-3 minutes.

4 Add the spinach and 75ml (2½fl oz) hot water. Cover and cook for 1 minute until tender, adding more hot water if the pan becomes dry.

5 Cook the noodles in the large pan of boiling water according to the packet instructions; drain.

6 Toss the vegetable mixture and parsley with the noodles. **Serve** immediately.

30 mins

vegetable hotpot & polenta

serves 4

300g (10½oz) granulated polenta

3 garlic cloves, sliced

2 onions, thinly sliced

4 courgettes, thinly sliced

225g (8oz) fresh green beans, cut in half

1 red pepper, finely sliced

1 green pepper, finely sliced

4 tomatoes, skinned, deseeded and roughly chopped

1 red chilli, cut into fine strips

1 tbsp extra virgin olive oil

salt and pepper

1 Heat the oil in a large pan and add the onions and garlic. Fry for 2 minutes then add all the vegetables and chilli.
2 Season and simmer for 25 minutes, stirring occasionally. Check the flavour and season to taste.
3 Meanwhile cook the polenta according to the packet instructions to make a soft mash.
Serve the vegetable hotpot on a bed of polenta mash.

Tip This dish also works well with polenta which is sliced and fried in butter and garlic. Sprinkle a little Tabasco sauce into the butter to add some bite!

30 mins

roasted field mushrooms

serves 4

8 large field mushrooms

salt and pepper

8 tsp green pesto

4 plum tomatoes, cut into 16 slices

5 tbsp olive oil

500g (1lb 2oz) packet ready-made polenta

bunch of fresh parsley, chopped

parmesan cheese, grated

1 Pre-heat the oven to 200°C/400°F/gas 6. Arrange the mushrooms in a roasting tin, gill side up, and roast for 10 minutes in the oven.

2 Remove from the oven, drain the juices into a bowl and set aside. Spoon pesto over each mushroom and lay two tomato slices on top.

3 Sprinkle the mushrooms with salt and pepper and 1 tbsp olive oil. Roast for a further 15 minutes.

4 Cut the polenta into wedges and fry on each side in the remaining oil until crisp and golden.

5 Sprinkle the mushrooms with grated parmesan and fresh chopped parsley and drizzle over the reserved mushroom juice.

Serve the mushrooms with the polenta and a salad.

main meals

30 mins

spatchcocked poussins

serves 4

4 single portion or 2 double portion poussins

4 tbsp tamarind pulp

150ml (5fl oz) tomato ketchup

4 tbsp clear honey

4 tbsp olive oil

juice of 2 lemons

1 To make the basting relish, mix the tamarind pulp, ketchup, honey, olive oil and lemon juice together.

2 Cut the poussins down the backbone with a pair of scissors and remove the backbone if possible. Flatten the poussins with the palm of your hand. Coat each one with the relish.

3 Thread a skewer diagonally from leg to opposite wing of each poussin and then repeat from the other side.

4 Barbecue for 20-25 minutes or until the juices from the legs run clear. Or cook in a pre-heated oven 220°C/450°F/gas 7 for 20 minutes. Do not cook poussins under a domestic grill as they tend to burn before being cooked through.
Serve on a bed of stir-fried vegetables tossed in a little soy sauce and sesame oil.

Tip Tamarind pulp is an oriental flavouring sold by the jar in most supermarkets. It gives a sour, tangy taste to sauces and curries. If you can't find it, use extra lemon juice instead.

chicken breasts with tarragon

30 mins

serves 4

4 x 175g (6oz) boneless, skinless chicken breasts

4 sprigs of fresh tarragon

2 tbsp plain flour

salt and pepper

25g (1oz) unsalted butter

1½ tbsp sunflower oil

2 shallots, finely chopped

225ml (8fl oz) dry white wine

350ml (12fl oz) chicken stock

4 tbsp crème fraîche

1 Pat the chicken dry with kitchen paper, dust with flour and season.

2 Heat the butter and 1 tbsp oil in a frying-pan over a moderate heat and fry the breasts for 5-6 minutes on each side. Keep the chicken warm.

3 Meanwhile, set aside 2 sprigs of tarragon for garnish. Strip the leaves from the other stems and chop coarsely.

4 Add the shallots to the pan with the rest of the oil and fry, stirring for 1 minute. Add the wine and half the chopped tarragon. Boil until the wine has reduced by half. Add the chicken stock and reduce by half again.

5 Stir in the crème fraîche and the remaining chopped tarragon, then return the chicken to the pan and warm it through for 1 minute on each side. Check the seasoning.

Serve with the sauce poured over the chicken and garnished with the tarragon sprigs. Plenty of warm French bread and a crisp salad go well with this simple dish.

30 mins

chicken with pink grapefruit & ginger

serves 4

4 boneless chicken breasts

1 pink grapefruit

2 pieces of stem ginger and 3 tbsp syrup taken from the jar

1 tbsp sunflower oil

2 garlic cloves, crushed

200ml (7fl oz) chicken stock

2 tbsp clear honey

sprigs of fresh parsley, to garnish

1 Pour the stem ginger syrup over the chicken and set it aside for as long as possible to marinate. Peel the grapefruit and cut away the pith. Cut between the membranes to release the segments. Cut the stem ginger into thin strips.

2 Heat the oil in a frying-pan over moderate heat and pan fry the chicken for 5 minutes on each side until a rich brown. Remove from the pan and set aside.

3 Add the garlic, stem ginger, chicken stock, honey and the syrup that the chicken was marinated in, to the pan. Bring to a simmer and cook for 2 minutes, stirring. Return the chicken to the pan; bring back to a simmer and leave to bubble for 5 minutes.

Serve the chicken with the grapefruit segments and covered with the sauce. Garnish with parsley sprigs.

25 mins

middle eastern chicken

serves 4

4 chicken breasts, boned and skinned

2 tsp ground coriander

1 tsp ground cumin

2 garlic cloves, crushed

1 tsp olive oil

140g (5oz) carton of set natural yoghurt

225g (8oz) basmati rice

4 vine tomatoes, chopped

½ cucumber, deseeded and chopped

4 tbsp chopped mint

6 spring onions, finely chopped

12 pitted black olives, sliced

juice of 1 lemon

salt and pepper

mint leaves, to garnish

lemon wedges, to garnish

1 Pre-heat the grill to medium. In a large mixing bowl, mix together the coriander, cumin, garlic, olive oil and yoghurt.
2 Add the chicken breasts to the yoghurt mixture and turn until they are coated.
3 Grill the breasts for 15-20 minutes, turning once, until just slightly charred.
4 Meanwhile, cook the rice for 10-12 minutes until just tender, then drain.
5 Mix the rice with the vine tomatoes, cucumber, mint, spring onions, black olives and lemon juice. Season to taste.
Serve on a bed of the rice tabbouleh. Garnish with mint leaves and lemon wedges.

30 mins

polenta crust chicken

serves 4

4 chicken breasts

6 tbsp instant polenta

salt and pepper

25g (1oz) plain flour

2 eggs, beaten

2 potatoes, finely grated and patted dry on a tea-towel

55g (2oz) canned sweetcorn, drained

1 onion, finely chopped

2 tbsp fresh parsley, chopped

vegetable oil for frying

6 tbsp tomato ketchup

lime slices to garnish

1 Season the flour and use to dust each chicken breast. Dip into the beaten egg, then into the polenta. Set aside for 5 minutes.

2 Mix the grated potato with the sweetcorn, half the onion and the parsley, then add enough of the beaten egg to bind the mix. Form the mix into 4 large loose patties.

3 Heat the vegetable oil in a large frying-pan, add the chicken breasts and cook over a medium heat for 10 minutes, turning, until golden brown.

4 Heat some more oil in another frying-pan, add the patties and cook for 3-4 minutes on each side until browned.

5 Mix the tomato ketchup with the rest of the onion.

Serve the chicken, carved into chunky slices, on top of the patties, with the oniony ketchup on the side. Garnish with lime slices and parsley.

chicken & vegetable stir-fry

25 mins

serves 4

4 chicken breasts, sliced

3 tbsp sesame oil

2 garlic cloves, crushed

1 small onion, finely chopped

3 red peppers, roughly chopped

200g (7oz) mangetout, rinsed

2 tbsp soy sauce

1 tbsp chicken stock

small bunch of flatleaf parsley, chopped

salt and pepper

1 Heat the wok or large frying-pan and add the oil. When the oil starts to smoke, add the garlic and onion. Stir-fry for a couple of minutes then add the chicken. Stir-fry for 7-8 minutes.

2 Add the pepper and mangetout and cook for 2 more minutes. Add the soy sauce and chicken stock and allow to simmer for 3 minutes. Add the parsley and season then cook for 2 more minutes.

Serve the chicken stir-fry with plain boiled rice.

Tip For a little added crunch, sprinkle in some toasted sesame seeds at the end.

25 mins

rosemary & lemon chicken kebabs

serves 4

675g (1½lb) chicken thighs

4 tbsp olive oil

zest and juice of 1 lemon

2 tbsp chopped rosemary

6 plum tomatoes, chopped

115g (4oz) feta cheese, crumbled

3 tbsp black olives

1 small red onion, chopped

1 tbsp olive oil

salt and pepper

pitta bread, toasted, to serve

1 Cut the chicken into 2.5cm (1in) cubes. Mix the cubes with the olive oil, lemon zest and juice, and rosemary.

2 Pre-heat the grill to high. Thread the chicken pieces on to 8 wooden skewers.

3 Grill the kebabs, turning frequently, for about 15 minutes until golden.

4 To make a Greek salad, mix together the plum tomatoes, feta cheese, black olives and red onion. Drizzle over the olive oil and season to taste.

Serve the kebabs on a bed of the Greek salad, with toasted pitta bread.

Tip **Soak the wooden skewers in water for a couple of hours to stop them from burning under the grill.**

turkey rolls with prosciutto & pesto

25 mins

serves 4

8 turkey breast steaks, about 85g (3oz) each

8 slices prosciutto

4 tbsp pesto

1 tbsp flour

8 slices of lemon

2 tbsp olive oil

125ml (4fl oz) white wine

55g (2oz) butter

1 Cover the turkey steaks with a sheet of plastic wrap and pound with a rolling pin until about 5mm (¼in) thick.
2 Remove the plastic wrap and spread each piece of turkey with pesto. Lay a slice of prosciutto on top and roll up. Dust with a little plain flour.
3 Place a slice of lemon on each roll, holding them in place with a cocktail stick.
4 Heat the oil in a frying-pan and fry the turkey rolls for 4 minutes, turning them regularly. Then pour in the wine and cook for 2 more minutes. Transfer the rolls from the pan to warm plates and remove the cocktail sticks.
5 Whisk the butter into the pan juices until it has melted. Then pour the sauce over the turkey rolls.
Serve with buttery new potatoes and snipped chives, green beans and baby carrots.

Tip If you can't find prosciutto, you can use thin rashers of cooked smoky bacon instead.

30 mins

creamy turkey & mushrooms

serves 4

450g (1lb) turkey breast stir-fry or turkey steaks, cut into strips

225g (8oz) button mushrooms, sliced

1 tbsp sunflower oil

75g (2¾oz) onions, chopped

55g (2oz) plain white flour

600ml (20fl oz) skimmed milk

1-2 tbsp horseradish sauce

2 tbsp chopped fresh parsley

salt and pepper

flatleaf parsley to garnish

1 Heat 1 tsp of the oil in a large frying-pan and sauté the onions for 4 minutes until softened but not browned.

2 Toss the turkey strips in 1 tsp of the oil. Add them to the onions in the pan and sauté for 5 minutes.

3 Add the remaining oil and the mushrooms and cook for 2-3 minutes more.

4 Sprinkle in the flour and cook for 1 minute. Gradually stir in the milk, scraping any residue from the bottom of the pan. Bring to the boil and cook for a further minute.

5 Reduce the heat to a simmer. Stir in the horseradish sauce to taste, parsley and seasoning. Simmer for a further 5 minutes.

Serve with mashed sweet potatoes, garnished with sprigs of parsley.

Tip Use wholegrain mustard if you prefer, rather than horseradish sauce.

crunchy coated lamb with lemon spinach

30 mins

serves 4

8 lamb chops, bones removed

juice and zest of 1 lemon

400g (14oz) spinach leaves, trimmed and washed

115g (4oz) fresh breadcrumbs

55g (2oz) pecorino cheese, finely grated

bunch flatleaf parsley, chopped

¼ tsp dried oregano

25g (1oz) flour

2 eggs, beaten

vegetable oil for shallow frying

1 garlic clove, crushed

6 tbsp olive oil

salt and pepper

pecorino shavings to garnish

fresh oregano to garnish

1 Pre-heat oven to 200°C/400°F/gas 6.

2 Mix the breadcrumbs, grated cheese, parsley, oregano and half the zest together and season.

3 Dip chops in seasoned flour and then the beaten egg. Coat in the breadcrumb mixture, patting down firmly.

4 Heat the oil for shallow frying. Brown the chops for 2-3 minutes on each side. Put in a roasting tin and cook for 8-10 minutes in the oven.

5 Mix lemon juice, garlic and 5 tbsp olive oil and season.

6 Heat 1 tbsp oil in a large pan and cook the spinach until it wilts. Toss in the lemon dressing and remaining zest.

Serve the lamb chops with the spinach on the side and garnish with pecorino shavings and fresh oregano.

30 mins

lamb chops with leek & pea confit

serves 4

4 double-loin lamb chops

450g (1lb) leeks, thinly sliced

150g (5oz) peas

400g (14oz) new potatoes

250g (9oz) unsalted butter

4 egg yolks

1 tsp Dijon mustard

1 small bunch of mint

1 tbsp oil

salt and pepper

1 Pre-heat the oven to 200°C/400°F/gas 6.

2 Boil the potatoes in boiling salted water for 10-15 minutes until tender.

3 To make a hollandaise sauce for the confit, melt 200g (7oz) butter in a small saucepan. Pulse the egg yolks, mustard and most of the mint in a food processor for 10 seconds. With the motor running, trickle in the melted butter to form a thick creamy sauce. Spoon into a bowl and set aside.

4 Place the chops in a roasting tin and season. Roast in the oven for 10-15 minutes.

5 Heat 25g (1oz) butter in a frying-pan and fry the leeks for 10 minutes until soft. Add peas and season. Cook for a further 5 minutes. Pre-heat the grill to high and drain the potatoes.

6 Top each chop with some leek and pea mixture and spoon on a little hollandaise.

7 Flash the chops under the grill for 10-15 seconds until the hollandaise is golden. Toss the potatoes with the rest of the butter and mint, then season.

Serve with the new potatoes.

lamb chops with spiced port sauce

30 mins

serves 4

8 lamb chops, trimmed

1kg (2½lb) potatoes, peeled and quartered

200g (7oz) green beans, trimmed

10-12 rosemary sprigs

1 tbsp oil

1 small onion, finely chopped

2 tbsp redcurrant jelly

2 tsp Worcestershire sauce

300ml (10fl oz) chicken stock

300ml (10fl oz) port

4 cloves and 1 bay leaf

3 tsp arrowroot in 3 tsp water

55g (2oz) butter

50ml (2fl oz) single cream

2 tsp coarse grain mustard

salt and pepper

1 Pre-heat the oven to 200°C/400°F/gas 6.

2 Boil the potatoes in salted water for 20 minutes until soft, then drain. Drop the beans into boiling water for 3 minutes, then drain.

3 Put the chops in a roasting tin and season. Sprinkle 8-10 rosemary sprigs over the chops and roast for 15-20 minutes.

4 Heat the oil in a sauté pan and fry the onion for 5 minutes. Add the jelly, Worcestershire sauce, stock, port, cloves and bay leaf. Simmer for 10 minutes.

5 Take the sauce off the heat and slowly stir in the arrowroot. Continue cooking gently until the sauce is thick and glossy.

6 Mash the potatoes with the butter, cream, mustard and seasoning until smooth.

Serve with mash and beans.

20 mins

steak with pepper sauce & cheese dip

serves 4

4 x 115-175g (4-6oz) fillet steaks

2 tbsp mixed peppercorns

100g (3½oz) Roquefort cheese

100g (3½oz) fine asparagus

25g (1oz) butter

salt and pepper

2 tbsp red wine

1 tsp red wine vinegar

4 tbsp single cream

1 tbsp crème fraîche

salad leaves to serve

1 Bring a pan of water to the boil and add the asparagus. Ideally stand the asparagus stalks on their ends and cover the pan so that the stalks are boiled and the tips are steamed to tenderness. Then drain and set aside.

2 Melt the butter in a large frying-pan. Season the steaks and add to the pan. Fry on each side until the steaks are cooked as you want. Remove the steak and place on a warm plate. Set aside to rest.

3 To make the sauce, add the peppercorns, red wine and vinegar to the residues in the pan, and mix well. Bring to the boil and simmer for 4-5 minutes until reduced.

4 Stir the cream into the pan. Season and simmer for 2 minutes. If you wish, crumble 25g (1oz) Roquefort into the sauce. Mash the rest with the crème fraîche.

Serve the steaks with the asparagus and salad, and the sauce drizzled round. Spoon a dollop of cheese dip on top.

30 mins

griddled steak with dijon new potatoes

serves 4

4 x 115-175g (4-6oz) fillet steaks

2 tbsp Dijon mustard

700g (1lb 9oz) small new potatoes, halved

2 tbsp white wine vinegar

200ml (7fl oz) olive oil

6 shallots, finely chopped

3 tbsp chopped fresh parsley

salt and pepper

55g (2oz) butter

1 Bring a large pan of salted water to the boil and add the potatoes. Cook for 12-15 minutes until just tender.
2 Meanwhile, whisk the mustard and vinegar together. Slowly add the oil, whisking continuously until you have a thick dressing.
3 Stir the shallots and the parsley into the dressing and season with salt and pepper.
4 Drain the potatoes and spoon over half the dressing. Set aside to cool slightly.
5 Season the steaks with lots of black pepper and melt the butter in a frying-pan. Cook the steaks to your own requirements.
Serve with the new potatoes and drizzle the rest of the dressing over them.

Tip You can use 2 tbsp of sun-dried tomato purée instead of Dijon mustard if you want a more robust Mediterranean flavour.

quick moussaka

25 mins

serves 4

350g (12oz) minced beef

350g (12oz) potatoes, cut into 1cm (½in) slices

1 aubergine, sliced into 1cm (½in) rounds

3 tbsp olive oil

1 small onion, chopped

1 garlic clove, crushed

200g (7oz) can chopped tomatoes

1 tbsp tomato purée

salt and pepper

2 tbsp fresh thyme, chopped

115g (4oz) gruyère cheese

1 packet mixed salad leaves

1 Pre-heat the grill. Boil the potatoes for 7-10 minutes until tender and drain. Lay the aubergine slices in a grill pan and brush with 1 tbsp of oil. Grill for 3-4 minutes, turn the slices over and brush with 1 tbsp oil. Grill for 3-4 minutes until golden and set aside.

2 Heat remaining oil in a frying-pan and add onion and garlic. Fry until softened and add the mince. Cook for 3 minutes. Pour off any excess liquid. Add tomatoes, tomato purée and seasoning. Simmer for 10 minutes until slightly thickened. Stir in half the thyme leaves.

3 Place mince in an ovenproof dish. Arrange aubergine over the mince. Top with potatoes. Sprinkle over the cheese and grill for 3-4 minutes until bubbling. Remove from grill and sprinkle with the rest of the thyme.

Serve from the cooking dish with a mixed salad.

beef in oyster sauce

15 mins

serves 4

450g (1lb) rump steak, finely sliced

2 tbsp oyster sauce

1 tbsp groundnut oil

2 garlic cloves, crushed

125g (4½oz) button mushrooms, sliced

1 tbsp sake or dry sherry

150ml (5fl oz) hot chicken stock

1 tsp brown sugar

½ red pepper, chopped

salt and pepper

1 tbsp cornflour mixed with 1 tbsp water

1 Heat the oil in a wok or deep frying-pan. Fry the garlic for about 1 minute until soft.
2 Add the steak and mushrooms and stir-fry for 2 minutes. Pour in the sake and cook for a further 2 minutes.
3 Add the stock, oyster sauce, sugar and red pepper, and season. Bring to the boil then simmer for 5 minutes until the beef is tender.
4 Stir in the cornflour paste and simmer for a further 3-5 minutes until the sauce thickens up.
Serve in deep bowls with boiled or steamed rice.

pork chops with sage & balsamic vinegar glaze

15 mins

serves 4

4 pork chops

4 sage leaves, finely chopped plus 12 for garnish

2 tbsp olive oil

2 tbsp balsamic vinegar

2 garlic cloves, crushed

3 tbsp Marsala

200ml (7fl oz) chicken stock

salt and pepper

25g (1oz) butter

400g (14oz) new potatoes

small bunch of chives, chopped

450g (1lb) cooked beetroot

1 Heat the olive oil in a large frying-pan. Brown the pork chops for 1 minute each side.

2 Meanwhile, cook the new potatoes in salted boiling water.

3 Add the garlic, balsamic vinegar and Marsala to the frying-pan. (The liquids sizzle and reduce immediately.) Add the stock and simmer for 10 minutes. Season then add the chopped sage and butter.

Serve each pork chop on a bed of mashed beetroot and with new potatoes sprinkled with chives. Garnish with sage leaves, cooled after being deep fried in hot oil for 10 seconds.

If you do not have Marsala, you can use sweet sherry or Madeira instead.

30 mins

braised pork chops with tomatoes & chickpeas

serves 4

4 pork chops

2 x 400g (14oz) cans
chopped tomatoes

400g (14oz) can chickpeas

4 tbsp oil

225g (8oz) onion, peeled
and finely chopped

3 garlic cloves, finely chopped

1 tbsp pimentón

2 tbsp anchovy essence

150ml (5fl oz) white wine

1 Heat the oil in a large frying-pan, add the pork chops and fry for 1 minute on each side, then remove from the pan.
2 Fry the onion for 5 minutes. Add the garlic and pimentón and cook for 2 minutes.
3 Add the tomatoes, anchovy essence and wine and bring to the boil. Simmer for 5 minutes.
4 Add the chickpeas and return the pork chops to the pan. Cook for 8-10 minutes, turning the chops over halfway through cooking.
Serve with some mixed salad leaves and crusty bread to mop up the juices. Garnish with chopped parsley.

pork chops with apples & cheese

30 mins

serves 4

4 pork chops

350g (12oz) eating apples, peeled, cored and quartered

250g (9oz) taleggio or bel paese cheese, rind removed, and sliced

55g (2oz) butter

115g (4oz) onion, peeled and finely chopped

25g (1oz) caster sugar

2 tbsp double cream

salt and pepper

450g (1lb) green beans

1 Pre-heat the oven to 200°C/400°F/gas 6.

2 Melt half the butter in a large frying-pan. Add the onion and fry for 5 minutes until golden.

3 Add the apples and sugar and cook for 10 minutes, stirring occasionally.

4 Meanwhile, place the pork chops in a roasting tin, dot with the remaining butter and roast in the hot oven for 10 minutes.

5 Transfer the apples and onions to an ovenproof dish, add the cream and season with salt and pepper. Arrange the pork chops on top and cover with slices of taleggio or bel paese cheese.

6 Return the dish to the oven and cook for a further 5-6 minutes. Then slide under a pre-heated grill for 2 minutes to brown the top.

7 Cook the green beans in lightly salted boiling water. **Serve** with the green beans.

30 mins

pork with tomato & peanut crust

serves 4

4 large pork chops

2 tbsp tomato purée

115g (4oz) peanuts

115g (4oz) long-grain rice

salt and pepper

2 tbsp olive oil

55g (2oz) breadcrumbs

bunch chives, snipped

lamb's lettuce, to serve

orange slices, to serve

1 Bring a large pan of salted water to the boil, add the rice and cook according to the packet instructions.
2 Pre-heat the grill to high. Season the pork chops and grill on one side only for 5-6 minutes.
3 Meanwhile blitz the peanuts, tomato purée, half the olive oil and the breadcrumbs to a chunky paste.
4 Remove the chops from the grill and spread the paste over the ungrilled side. Put back under the grill, paste side up, for 5-6 minutes, and grill until the pork chops are cooked through thoroughly and the peanut crust is golden.
5 Drain the cooked rice and toss with the remainder of the oil. Add the snipped chives and toss again.
Serve the pork chops with the rice and lamb's lettuce on the side, garnished with a slice of orange.

25 mins

gammon with broad bean sauce

serves 4

4 x 200g (7oz) gammon steaks

300g (10oz) can broad beans, drained and rinsed

25g (1oz) butter

25g (1oz) flour

300ml (10fl oz) milk

2 tbsp double cream

1 tbsp chopped flatleaf parsley

1 tbsp chopped fresh tarragon

salt and pepper

creamy mashed potatoes to serve

1 Melt the butter in a non-stick saucepan. Add the flour and cook for 1 minute. Slowly add the milk, stirring all the time, to make a smooth sauce. Season and cook for 5 minutes.

2 Place the gammon steaks on a grill pan and cook under a pre-heated grill for about 3-4 minutes.

4 Add the beans, cream and herbs to the sauce and heat through.

Serve the herby broad bean sauce with the gammon steaks and creamy mashed potatoes.

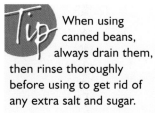

Tip When using canned beans, always drain them, then rinse thoroughly before using to get rid of any extra salt and sugar.

pork, apple & sage kebabs

30 mins

serves 4

550g (1¼lb) pork fillet, cut into 16 cubes

2 eating apples, sliced into 16 segments

16 large sage leaves

1 garlic clove, crushed

2 tbsp olive oil

1 tsp crushed fennel seeds

2 tbsp cider

1 tbsp honey

salt and pepper

crusty bread to serve

sage leaves to garnish

1 Pre-heat the grill to high. Thread the pork, apple and sage leaves on to 4 skewers. Sit the skewers in the bottom of a shallow dish.

2 To make the marinade, mix the garlic, olive oil, fennel seeds, cider, honey and seasoning in a small bowl.

3 Pour the marinade over the skewers and marinate the kebabs for 5-10 minutes.

4 Then grill or barbecue the kebabs for 10-12 minutes until the pork is cooked and has a sticky glaze.

Serve with crusty bread on the side and garnish with sage.

 For vegetarians, substitute 2.5cm (1in) cubes of halloumi cheese for the pork. Marinate the cheese as above. Then thread the cubes on to the skewers and grill or barbecue, also as above.

30 mins

pork sausages with porcini mushrooms

serves 4

450g (1lb) good-quality sausages, skinned, or sausagemeat

40g (1½oz) dried porcini mushrooms, soaked in boiling water for 10 minutes

½ bunch fresh marjoram

1 garlic clove, crushed

175g (6oz) shallots, sliced

3 tbsp olive oil

200ml (7fl oz) red wine

1 tbsp tomato paste

1 tsp balsamic vinegar

1 tsp Worcestershire sauce

salt and pepper

1 Chop the marjoram and garlic, mix into the meat and pack on to the skewers.

2 Place the sausage skewers under a grill or on a barbecue for 10-15 minutes until golden, turning occasionally.

3 Meanwhile gently fry the shallots in oil for 10 minutes until soft. Add the wine and boil to reduce by half. Add the mushrooms and their soaking liquor, avoiding any grit from the bottom. Add the other ingredients and bubble for 5 minutes until the sauce is thick and glossy.

Serve two skewers each with the sauce poured over them. Eat with buttery garlic mashed potatoes and a fresh green salad.

sausages with lentils & onion

25 mins

serves 4

8 pork sausages

200g (7oz) can green lentils

1 medium onion, finely chopped

2 garlic cloves, crushed

1 tbsp olive oil

25g (1oz) butter

85g (3oz) bacon, cut in strips

1 tsp caster sugar

½ tsp dried thyme

100g (3½oz) jar sun-dried tomatoes, drained and chopped

100g (3½oz) baby spinach leaves

salt and pepper

1 Heat the oil in a large frying-pan and add the onion and garlic. Fry the sausages for 10-15 minutes to brown them on all sides. Once the sausages are done, remove them from the pan and cut into bite-sized pieces.

2 Meanwhile melt the butter in a clean pan and fry the bacon and sprinkle in the sugar. Stir until the bacon is frizzled.

3 With a slotted spoon, transfer the sausages, onions and garlic to the bacon pan.

4 Drain the lentils, rinse under cold water and stir into the sausage mixture with the sun-dried tomatoes and thyme.

5 Cook until the lentils and sausages are heated through. Finally stir in the spinach and heat until it has just wilted, then season.

Serve with Dijon mustard and crusty bread.

30 mins

sausages & red cabbage in red wine

serves 4

8 pork sausages

1 red cabbage, sliced

3 tbsp red wine

100g (3½ oz) butter

1 red onion, sliced

2 shallots, chopped

55g (2oz) juniper berries

1 tbsp red wine vinegar

1 tsp caster sugar

salt and pepper

1 Pre-heat the oven to 140°C/275°F/gas 1.

2 Melt the butter in a heavy based frying-pan. Add the onion and shallots and cook for 2 minutes until slightly soft. Add the sausages and fry for 10-15 minutes, turning regularly until cooked evenly.

3 Remove the sausages from the pan and put them in the oven to keep warm.

4 Add the cabbage to the pan and sweat for 5 minutes. Stir in the juniper berries, vinegar, red wine, sugar and seasoning. Simmer for 10 minutes, stirring occasionally, until the liquid is completely absorbed.

Serve the sausages on top of a bed of cabbage.

Tip Cranberries also make a colourful addition to this dish. Use them as a sweeter alternative to the juniper berries.

25 mins

grilled cod with lemon butter sauce

serves 4

4 x 175-225g (6-8oz) cod fillets, skinned

25g (1oz) softened butter

115g (4oz) unsalted butter, chilled and diced

1½-2 tbsp lemon juice

2 tbsp chicken or vegetable stock

salt and pepper

1 Set the grill to medium-hot. Brush a baking tray or grill pan with oil. Season the cod fillets well on both sides and brush with the softened butter. Place on the baking tray or grill pan and grill for 8-10 minutes on one side.

2 While the fish is cooking, place the unsalted butter, lemon juice and stock in a small pan and bring to a simmer over a low heat, whisking continuously. (Do not let the sauce boil or it will separate.)

3 Pour the sauce over the cod fillets, sharing it out equally between the four portions.

Serve with buttered new potatoes and a green salad.

Tip For an extra creamy finish to the sauce, blitz the butter, lemon juice and stock together with a hand blender.

open cod hash with spring onions

30 mins

serves 4

750g (1½lb) cod fillet, skinned and cut in 2.5cm (1in) chunks

450g (1lb) new potatoes in skins

2-3 tbsp olive oil

55g (2oz) butter

1 large bunch spring onions, roughly chopped

1 tsp plain flour

salt and pepper

squeeze of lemon juice

1 Cut the potatoes into quarters, put them in boiling water and cook for 15 minutes. Drain, cool in cold, running water and peel.
2 Heat 1 tbsp olive oil and 25g (1oz) butter in a frying-pan. Add the potato and spring onion. Fry until the potato is golden, then add the spring onion and cook for a further 3 minutes. Season.
3 Dust the cubes of cod with lightly seasoned flour. Heat the remaining oil and butter in another pan and fry the cod cubes for 5-6 minutes turning until golden brown.
4 Add the potatoes and spring onions to the frying-pan – the fish breaks into flakes while the potatoes stay whole.
Serve with a squeeze of lemon juice.

Tip For a softer, cake-like hash, use boiled, old-crop potatoes and mash them lightly before frying with the cod.

lemon sole & chunky chips

30 mins

serves 4

4 lemon sole fillets, halved lengthways

8 potatoes

100g (3½oz) plain flour

salt and freshly ground black pepper

1 tbsp olive oil

finely grated rind of 1 lemon

2 tbsp finely chopped dill

vegetable oil for deep frying

whites of 2 small eggs

coarse sea salt and mayonnaise, to serve

1 Sift the flour and seasoning into a large bowl. Make a well in the centre and whisk in the olive oil and 150ml (5fl oz) water until a smooth batter is formed. Stir in the lemon rind and chopped dill. Set aside.

2 Peel the potatoes and cut them into chips.

3 Heat the oil in a large pan. While it's heating, whisk the egg whites until stiff and then fold them into the batter.

4 Test the oil temperature by pouring a drop of the batter into the pan; if the batter floats and the oil bubbles around its edges, the oil is hot enough. Dip the lemon sole into the batter and then deep fry, 2 pieces at a time, for 3-4 minutes until the batter is golden. Drain on kitchen paper and keep warm.

5 Deep fry the chips in the hot oil for 6 minutes until crisp. Drain on kitchen paper.

Serve sprinkled with the sea salt and with a green salad and a good dollop of mayonnaise.

25 mins

baked fish with a lime crust

serves 4

900g (2lb) fish fillet cut into 4 equal pieces

finely grated zest of 4 limes or 9 kaffir lime leaves, finely shredded

150g (5½oz) butter

115g (4oz) fresh white breadcrumbs

juice of 4 limes

bunch of fresh parsley, finely chopped

salt and pepper

green salad to serve

1 Pre-heat the oven to 220°C/425°F/gas 7. Rub a little of the butter over the base of an ovenproof dish just large enough for the fish fillets to sit snugly side by side.

2 Mix the breadcrumbs with the lime zest or lime leaves in a small bowl. Reserve 1 tbsp of parsley and mix the rest into the breadcrumbs. Season well.

3 Place the fish in the ovenproof dish. Squeeze the juice of 2 limes over the fish and scatter with the crumbs, pressing down lightly. Dot with butter and bake in the pre-heated oven for 15 minutes until the crumbs are crisp and golden brown.

4 Place the fillets on warm plates. Add the remaining parsley and lime juice to the ovenproof dish and mix with the buttery juices, then spoon over the fish.

Serve with a fresh crisp green salad.

haddock, leek & cheesy bake

30 mins

serves 4

700g (1lb 9oz) smoked haddock fillets, skinned and boned

175g (6oz) leeks, sliced

300ml ready-made cheese sauce

150ml (5fl oz) milk

225g (8oz) potatoes, cut into 1cm (½in) cubes

2 hard-boiled eggs, roughly chopped

2 tbsp capers

175g (6oz) fresh white breadcrumbs

2 tbsp chopped parsley

25g (1oz) butter

1 Pre-heat the oven to 200°C/400°F/gas 6. Heat the milk in a frying-pan. Add the fish and poach for 3-4 minutes. Remove the fish and flake into small pieces.

2 Meanwhile, bring a large pan of water to the boil and add the potatoes and leeks. Boil for 2 minutes then drain.

3 Heat the cheese sauce in a large pan. Add the potatoes, leeks, fish, egg and capers to the cheese sauce and mix. Pour into a large ovenproof dish. Scatter the breadcrumbs and half the parsley over.

4 Dot the butter around the top of the dish. Cook for 20 minutes in the oven until breadcrumbs are crispy.

Serve with the rest of the fresh parsley scattered over and a serving of green beans.

crunchy smoked fish pie

30 mins

serves 4

400g packet filo pastry

250g (9oz) cooked smoked haddock, broken into chunks

115g (4oz) butter

55g (2oz) plain flour

600ml (1 pint) milk

salt and pepper

115g (4oz) frozen peas, thawed

100g (3oz) can sweetcorn, drained

25g (1oz) melted butter

25g (1oz) sesame seeds

1 Pre-heat the oven to 200°C/400°F/gas 6. Melt the butter in a heavy-based saucepan and add the flour. Stir with a wooden spoon to form a roux. Gradually add the milk to create a smooth white sauce. Season well.

2 Add the haddock to the sauce with the peas and sweetcorn and pile the mixture into a pie dish.

3 Brush the melted butter over the pastry sheets and layer them over the fish, scrunching the top. Scatter with sesame seeds and bake for 15 minutes until the pastry is golden.

Serve with a green vegetable.

Tip To get the rosette effect with filo, cut the sheets into three and roll into loose flowery shapes. Arrange rosettes on top of pie and bake as before.

30 mins

red mullet with rosemary

serves 4

1.1kg (2½lb) red mullet, scaled, gutted and cleaned

1 tbsp finely chopped rosemary

3 tbsp olive oil

juice of 2 lemons

salt and pepper

8 sprigs rosemary

1 Lightly score the red mullet with a sharp knife, then place them in a shallow bowl.
2 Whisk together the rosemary, olive oil and lemon juice, then season. Pour over the mullet and leave to marinate for 10 minutes.
3 Remove the fish from the marinade. Put them in a fish clamp, or straight on to the barbecue grill, with the sprigs of rosemary.
4 Barbecue for 16-18 minutes, turning once, and basting frequently with any remaining marinade.
Serve with barbecued vegetables and a green salad.

Tip To prevent the fish from sticking, brush the fish clamp or barbecue grill with oil before barbecuing.

sicilian monkfish kebabs

20 mins

serves 4

900g (2lb) monkfish fillet, cut into 24 cubes

16 sage leaves

150ml (5fl oz) extra virgin olive oil

1 garlic clove, crushed

2 tbsp lemon juice

1 tsp sugar

1 tbsp chopped parsley

1 tbsp chopped basil

salt and pepper

400g (14oz) tagliatelle

oregano sprigs to garnish

1 Bring a large pan of salted water to the boil. Drop in the pasta and cook until tender. Pre-heat the grill to medium.
2 Thread the monkfish cubes on to 8 skewers with a sage leaf between each cube.
3 In a small bowl whisk all but 2 tbsp of the olive oil, the garlic, lemon juice, sugar, herbs and seasoning with 3 tbsp of hot water.
4 Brush the olive oil mixture liberally over the monkfish. Grill the fish on skewers for 5 minutes on either side.
5 Drain the pasta and toss it in the remaining olive oil.
Serve the skewers with the tagliatelle. Drizzle the remaining olive oil mixture over the kebabs and garnish with small sprigs of oregano.

 Give the dressing an extra spark by adding a little finely grated lemon zest with the herbs.

30 mins

peppered tuna with coriander seeds

serves 4

4 tuna steaks

1½ tbsp black peppercorns, crushed

7 tsp coriander seeds, crushed

2 small red onions, roughly sliced

8 plum tomatoes, peeled, deseeded and quartered

225ml (8fl oz) olive oil

½ tsp salt

juice of 1 lemon

2 tbsp roughly chopped fresh coriander

125g (4½oz) rocket leaves

1 Pre-heat the grill to high. Mix the red onions and tomatoes with 2 tbsp oil, 1 tsp crushed coriander seeds and the salt. Spread in a shallow flameproof dish and grill for 8 minutes, turning occasionally.

2 Transfer to a large bowl and stir in 100ml (3½fl oz) oil and the lemon juice. Set aside for 10 minutes.

3 Heat a griddle pan over high heat. Brush the tuna with the remaining oil – don't worry if you don't use up all the oil. Mix the remaining coriander seeds with the peppercorns and coat both sides of the tuna. Griddle the tuna for 2-3 minutes on each side.

4 Stir the fresh coriander into the red onion mixture and spoon a little into the centre of individual serving plates. Pile some rocket leaves on top of this, reserving a few for garnish. Top each pile of leaves with a tuna steak, cut in half.

Serve garnished with rocket.

fresh trout with walnut dressing

15 mins

serves 4

4 trout fillets

10 walnut halves

1 shallot, finely chopped

1 tbsp finely chopped dill

2 tbsp spiced rice vinegar

6 tbsp walnut oil

salt and pepper

1 tsp vegetable oil

¼ tsp paprika

125g (4½oz) watercress, rocket or mixed salad leaves

1 Pre-heat the grill to high. To make the dressing, mix together the shallot, dill, vinegar and walnut oil, and season to taste.

2 Line the grill pan with foil. Oil it with half the vegetable oil and lay the fillets, skin side down, on top and sprinkle with paprika.

3 Grill the fillets for 6-8 minutes until brown at the edges but pink in the centre.

4 Meanwhile, heat the rest of the oil in a small frying-pan and gently fry the walnuts, stirring constantly, until they colour.

5 Remove the walnuts from the pan, drain on kitchen paper, then chop coarsely.

6 Arrange the salad leaves on 4 plates. Lay a fillet on each plate. Spoon the dressing over the fillets and scatter with the chopped walnuts.

Serve with boiled new potatoes tossed in a little butter and dill.

15 mins

pan-fried almond trout

serves 4

4 trout fillets

8 tbsp flaked almonds

12 tbsp fresh white breadcrumbs

zest of 1 lemon

2 tbsp flour

salt and pepper

2 eggs, beaten

55g (2oz) butter

2 tbsp olive oil

1 lemon, cut into wedges

1 Mix together the breadcrumbs, almonds and lemon zest on a plate.
2 Season the flour. Dip the trout fillets into the flour and then into the beaten egg.
3 Thoroughly coat each fillet in the almond and breadcrumb mixture.
4 Heat the butter and olive oil in a deep frying-pan. Fry the fillets for about 8 minutes, turning once, until crisp and golden brown.
Serve with wedges of lemon and a green salad.

Tip This is a good recipe to serve to children as the fillets are bone-free.

herby salmon on mash

20 mins

serves 4

4 salmon fillets

6 tbsp finely chopped fresh mixed herbs

900g (2lb) floury potatoes, peeled and cut into equal sizes

1 red pepper, de-seeded and cut in quarters

75ml (2½fl oz) milk

115g (4oz) crème fraîche

55g (2oz) butter

3 tbsp white wine

salt and pepper

1 Pre-heat the grill to hot. Grill the pepper until the skin blackens, then place in a plastic bag to cool. Peel and finely dice.

2 Bring a large pan of salted water to the boil and add the potatoes. Boil for 10-12 minutes until tender. Drain the potatoes, add the milk and crème fraîche, then mash and season to taste.

3 Roll the salmon fillets in the herbs and season. Melt the butter in a frying-pan. Add the salmon, reduce the heat and fry for 2-3 minutes on each side. Add the wine and cook for another 3-4 minutes.

4 Remove the fish and add the pepper to the pan. Heat through gently.

Serve the fish on a bed of mash, topped with the pepper and pan juices.

salmon with butter bean purée

15 mins

serves 4

- 4 x 150g (5oz) salmon fillets
- 2 x 400g (7oz) cans butter beans, drained and rinsed
- 1 garlic clove, peeled
- zest and juice of 1 lemon
- 2 tbsp mayonnaise
- 6 tbsp olive oil
- 15g (½oz) fresh basil
- salt and pepper
- radicchio leaves
- 500g (1lb 2oz) pkt noodles

1 Blitz the butter beans with the garlic, lemon zest and juice, salt and pepper and mayonnaise.

2 With the blender still running, add 5 tbsp of the olive oil and process to a smooth purée. If the mixture looks a bit stiff, add 2-3 tbsp water. Transfer to a small non-stick pan and heat gently.

3 Tear the basil leaves into pieces and fold gently into the purée. (Reserve some whole leaves for garnishing the salmon.)

4 Put noodles on to cook.

5 Heat the remaining oil in a frying-pan and add the salmon fillets. Cook on each side for 2-3 minutes until pale pink and just ready to flake.

Serve the salmon on the warm butter bean purée accompanied by radicchio and buttered noodles.

Tip Butter bean purée makes a delicious dip for crudités. Finely chop rather than tear the basil leaves.

salmon goujons with tartare sauce

30 mins

serves 4

450g (1lb) salmon fillet

1 egg

1 tbsp olive oil

7 tbsp beer

5 tbsp plain flour

8 tbsp mayonnaise

1 tbsp chopped capers

1 tbsp chopped green olives

2 tbsp chopped fresh parsley

2 tsp lemon juice

vegetable oil for deep frying

lemon wedges, to serve

1 Separate the egg. Make a batter by beating together the egg yolk, olive oil, beer and flour. Set aside.

2 To make the tartare sauce, mix together the mayonnaise, capers, olives, parsley and lemon juice. Then cut the salmon into strips.

3 Heat the oil in a large pan. While it's getting hot, whisk the egg white until stiff and then fold into the batter.

4 Test the temperature of the oil by pouring a drop of the batter into the pan; if the batter floats and the oil bubbles around its edges, the oil is hot enough. Dip the strips of salmon into the batter and deep fry in the hot oil, in batches if necessary, for about 2 minutes or until golden.

Serve with the tartare sauce and lemon wedges, accompanied by some crisp and fresh green vegetables, such as broccoli or mangetouts.

salmon & vegetable parcels

30 mins

serves 4

16 sheets of filo pastry, about 15 x 30cm (6 x 12in)

4 small salmon fillets

55g (2oz) broccoli florets

55g (2oz) cauliflower florets

1 red pepper, cut into wide strips

2 carrots, cut into wide strips

1 leeks, cut into wide strips

85g (3oz) butter, melted

1 tbsp lemon juice

1 tsp grainy mustard

1 Steam the vegetables for 5 minutes until softened. Grill the salmon fillets for about 10 minutes until cooked. Cover with foil and keep warm.

2 Pre-heat the oven to 180°C/350°F/gas 4.

3 Lay out one sheet of pastry and brush with some of the melted butter. Top with three more sheets of filo pastry, brushing each one with more melted butter.

4 Place a salmon fillet at one end of the rectangle. Lay a quarter of the lightly steamed vegetables around the salmon fillet. Carefully roll up the filo pastry. Repeat until you have four parcels.

5 Place the parcels on a lightly greased baking tray and brush with melted butter. Bake for 10-15 minutes until golden brown and crispy.

6 To make a butter sauce, whisk the lemon juice and grainy mustard into the remaining butter.

Serve each parcel in a pool of the sauce with new potatoes.

30 mins

salmon, seafood & green bean stew

serves 4

500g (1lb 2oz) salmon, skinned and boned

125g (4½oz) cooked peeled prawns

150g (5½oz) green beans, halved

1 tbsp olive oil

150g (5½oz) carrots, thickly sliced

2 celery sticks, sliced

150g (5½oz) onions, sliced

1 garlic clove, crushed

350g (12oz) new potatoes

300ml (10fl oz) fish stock

10-12 strands of saffron

125ml (4fl oz) dry white wine

1 tbsp cornflour

1 tbsp skimmed milk

salt and black pepper

1 tbsp chopped fresh chives

sprigs of thyme, to serve

1 Heat the oil in a large pan and add the carrots, celery and onions. Cover and cook over low heat for 5 minutes.

2 Add the garlic and potatoes and cook, uncovered, for 5 minutes, stirring occasionally.

3 Add the stock and saffron. Cover and simmer for 10 minutes.

4 Meanwhile, cut the fish into 4cm (1½in) chunks. Add the fish, beans and wine to the pan. Cover and simmer for another 5 minutes.

5 Mix the cornflour and milk; stir in with the prawns. Cook until the stew thickens slightly and the prawns are warm. Season and stir in the chives.

Serve sprinkled with thyme.

25 mins

mussels with fennel & vermouth

serves 4

2kg (4½lb) live mussels, cleaned

1 large head fennel

175ml (6fl oz) dry vermouth

25g (1oz) butter

150g (5½oz) onions, chopped

1 garlic clove, chopped

1 tbsp chopped fresh parsley

black pepper

1 Dice the fennel and finely chop the fronds – set these aside. Melt the butter in a large saucepan and add the diced fennel, onions and garlic. Cover and cook gently for 10 minutes until the vegetables are tender.

2 Stir in the vermouth, parsley, fennel fronds and black pepper and bring to the boil. Add the mussels, cover and cook for 4-5 minutes, shaking the pan occasionally, until the mussels have opened. Discard any that do not open.

3 Transfer the mussels to individual serving bowls and pour the hot cooking liquor over them.

Serve with plenty of fresh crusty bread to mop up all the mussel-flavoured juices.

Tip If you don't have a large enough saucepan for all the mussels, use two pans and divide the ingredients between them.

asparagus & gruyère tarts

30 mins

serves 4

250g (9oz) asparagus tips

50g (1¾oz) gruyère, grated

250g (9oz) ready-made shortcrust pastry

2 egg yolks

200g (7oz) crème fraîche

1 Pre-heat the oven to 200°C/400°F/gas 6. Roll out the pastry and use to line four 10cm (4in) tartlet tins; set aside to chill briefly.

2 Meanwhile, steam the asparagus for 3-4 minutes until tender. Then bake the pastry cases blind for 10 minutes.

3 Set aside four tips of the cooked asparagus, about 7.5cm (3in) long, and then roughly chop up the rest. Mix the chopped asparagus with the egg yolks, crème fraîche and gruyère.

4 Reduce the oven to 160°C/325°F/gas 3. Divide the asparagus mixture between the pastry cases. Top each with a reserved asparagus tip and bake for 20 minutes until golden and nearly set.

Serve once the tarts have cooled slightly and set more firmly. Accompany with a simple green salad.

goat's cheese & vegetable tart

25 mins

serves 4

100g (3½oz) goat's cheese log, sliced

1 small aubergine, chopped

1 courgette, chopped

1 red pepper, deseeded and chopped

2 tomatoes, chopped

375g (13oz) packet ready-rolled puff pastry

6 tbsp olive oil

115g (4oz) pitted black olives

salt and pepper

1 egg, beaten

1 packet green salad

1 tbsp balsamic vinegar

1 Pre-heat the oven to 200°C/400°F/gas 6.

2 Cut the pastry into four pieces. Score 1cm (½in) inside the edge with a knife to form a rim. Place the rectangles on two baking trays.

3 Heat 2 tbsp olive oil in a large frying-pan and add all the vegetables, olives and seasoning. Fry for 5 minutes.

4 Spoon the filling on to the centre of each pastry rectangle. Brush the edge with the egg. Drizzle 1 tbsp olive oil on top.

5 Arrange the goat's cheese slices on top of the tart so that they will not melt over the pastry and prevent it from rising. Bake for 15 minutes.

6 Whisk 3 tbsp olive oil and 1 tbsp balsamic vinegar together, season and toss with the green salad.

Serve one tart per person with the green salad, pouring a little extra olive oil on to the tarts if liked.

onion & shallot pastries with salad

20 mins

serves 4

2 red onions, thinly sliced

4 shallots, quartered

250g (9oz) ready-rolled puff pastry

1 egg, beaten

12 sprigs of fresh thyme

4 tbsp olive oil

salt and pepper

55g (2oz) stilton

3 tbsp whipping cream

1 tbsp walnut oil

1 tsp sherry vinegar

85g (3oz) baby spinach leaves, washed and trimmed

85g (3oz) watercress, washed and trimmed

25g (1oz) walnut pieces, roughly chopped

1 Pre-heat oven to 220°C/425°F/gas 7.
2 Cut out four 15cm (6in) rounds from the pastry. Place on a baking sheet and brush with beaten egg.
3 Divide onions and shallots between each pastry disc, leaving a 2cm (¾in) border all round. Place 3 thyme sprigs on top. Brush the onions and shallots with olive oil and season. Bake for 20 minutes.
4 Meanwhile, mash the stilton and whipping cream together in another bowl with a fork. Beat walnut oil and sherry vinegar into the stilton cream and season with pepper. Drizzle over the spinach, watercress and walnut pieces in a large salad bowl and toss.
Serve the hot pastries with the salad.

wild mushroom risotto parcels

30 mins

serves 4

16 sheets of filo pastry, cut into 25cm (10in) squares

150g (5½oz) wild mushrooms, chopped

100g (3½oz) mixed rice grains

7 tbsp olive oil

100g (3½oz) mangetout, diced

55g (2oz) parmesan, grated

2 tbsp chopped basil

55g (2oz) butter, melted

4 long chives

1 red pepper, finely diced

1 yellow pepper, finely diced

1 tbsp lemon juice

1 Pre-heat the oven to 180°C/350°F/gas 4. Cook the rice according to the packet instructions. Drain.

2 Heat 1 tbsp oil and fry the mushrooms for 2 minutes. Add the mangetout and fry for 2 minutes. Then stir into the cooked rice with the parmesan and basil.

3 Layer 4 squares on top of each other, brushing each with melted butter. Repeat until there are 4 layered squares.

4 Spoon a quarter of the rice mixture into the centre of each square. Draw up the edges and pinch together.

5 Brush with melted butter and bake for 10-15 minutes. Allow to cool, then tie a chive round the neck of each parcel.

6 Make a pepper dressing by mixing together the peppers, the rest of the olive oil and lemon juice.

Serve the parcels drizzled with the pepper dressing.

30 mins

cheesy potato & vegetable hotpot

serves 4

500g (1lb 2oz) small new potatoes, washed and sliced

1 large onion, chopped

2 garlic cloves, crushed

2 courgettes, sliced

2 red peppers, diced

2 green peppers, diced

4 tomatoes, chopped

85g (3oz) butter

salt and pepper

115g (4oz) cheddar cheese, grated

1 Bring a large pan of salted water to the boil and add the potatoes. Boil for 5-6 minutes until just tender.

2 Meanwhile melt half the butter in a large frying-pan and add the onion and garlic. Fry gently until softened, then add the courgettes, peppers, tomatoes and seasoning. Cook over a medium heat for 10-12 minutes until softened.

3 Drain the potatoes as soon as they are ready. Add the remaining butter to a smaller frying-pan and heat until it is frothing. Add the potato slices and fry on either side until slightly browned.

4 Arrange the potatoes on top of the cooked vegetables in the large frying-pan and sprinkle the cheese over them. Season well. Place under the grill for 2-3 minutes until the cheese is melted and bubbling. **Serve** the potatoes and vegetables straight from the pan.

spinach & ricotta filo pie

30 mins

serves 4

400g (14oz) packet filo pastry
450g (1lb) baby spinach
300g (10½oz) ricotta cheese
1 tsp ground nutmeg
1 tbsp olive oil
1 onion, finely chopped
3 tomatoes, cut in eighths
55g (2oz) black olives, pitted
salt and pepper
25g (1oz) butter, melted
grated parmesan to serve (optional)

1 Pre-heat the oven to 200°C/400°F/gas 6.

2 Pour boiling water over the spinach in a colander until it is wilted. Squeeze all the water out of the leaves and tip them into a bowl.

3 Crumble the ricotta into the bowl and mash into the spinach with a fork. Add the nutmeg and season.

4 Heat the oil in a frying-pan and add the onion. Fry until just softened, then add the tomatoes and olives. Season and fry for 2-3 minutes.

5 Gently mix the onion, tomatoes and olives into the bowl of spinach and ricotta. Place the pie filling in a dish.

6 Brush the pastry sheets with the melted butter. Arrange the sheets to cover the filling, scrunching up the top layer.

7 Bake in the oven for 15 minutes until the pastry is golden and very crisp.

Serve the pie with grated parmesan if you wish.

30 mins

baked eggs, spinach & mushrooms

serves 4

4 large eggs

225g (8oz) fresh spinach, washed and well drained

115g (4oz) button mushrooms, sliced

55g (2oz) butter

salt and pepper

pinch of grated nutmeg

4 tbsp double cream

85g (3oz) gruyère cheese, grated

1 Heat 25g (1oz) butter in a wok or large frying-pan and add spinach. Cook for 2-3 minutes until it just wilts. Place in a mixing bowl and season with salt, pepper and nutmeg.

2 Wipe out pan and heat rest of butter. Add mushrooms and fry for 3-4 minutes.

3 Arrange spinach and mushrooms in 4 gratin dishes. Make a hollow in the centre and crack an egg into each.

4 Pour 1 tbsp of cream over each egg. Sprinkle with cheese.

5 Bake in a pre-heated oven at 180°C/350°F/gas 4 for 12-15 minutes until the yolks and whites are set.

Serve with crusty bread.

Tip If you prefer, you can bake all the eggs in one large gratin dish rather than individual ones. Use cheddar if you don't have any gruyère.

cheesy soufflé omelette with cress

30 mins

serves 4

8 eggs

225g (8oz) cheddar cheese, grated

small bunch of cress

55g (2oz) butter

1 onion, thinly sliced into rings

4 tbsp double cream

1 tsp English mustard powder

salt and pepper

2 tbsp mustard seeds

tomato salad and crusty white bread to serve

1 Heat half the butter in a frying-pan and add the onion rings. Fry for 6-7 minutes until slightly golden.

2 Separate the egg yolks and whites. Beat the yolks with half the cheese, the double cream, mustard powder and seasoning.

3 Whisk the egg whites until stiff. Fold the yolk mixture into the fluffy whites.

4 Melt the remaining butter into a large heavy-based frying-pan and add the egg mixture. (If your pan is not big enough, you may have to cook two large omelettes instead of a single huge one.)

5 Cook for 3-4 minutes until the bottom is golden, then scatter the fried onion rings and the extra cheese on top.

6 Grill the top of the omelette until golden and puffed up. Scatter the mustard seeds and cress over and fold in half. Slice the omelette into 2 or 4 pieces and place on the plates. **Serve** with a tomato salad and crusty white bread.

mushroom omelette with garlic butter

15 mins

serves 4

6 eggs

400g (14oz) chanterelle or brown cap mushrooms, wiped clean

175g (6oz) crème fraîche

2 tbsp chopped chives

salt and pepper

55g (2oz) butter

2 leeks, trimmed and sliced

2 garlic cloves, crushed

1 tsp grated nutmeg

2 tbsp lemon juice

1 Mix the crème fraîche and chives together and season. In a separate bowl, beat the eggs together with a little seasoning and set aside.

2 Heat half the butter in a frying-pan and sauté the leeks and garlic together until softened. Add the mushrooms and fry for 3-4 minutes. Add the nutmeg and lemon juice to the leeks and season.

3 Melt half the remaining butter in a large frying-pan. Add half the beaten eggs and swirl out to the edges of the pan. Once the eggs begin to set, add half the mushroom and leek mixture and half the crème fraîche and chives.

4 Fold the omelette over and cook for a further 10-15 seconds. Slide the omelette out of the pan and keep warm while cooking the second omelette.

Serve half of each omelette as a portion with a green salad and garlic bread on the side.

20 mins

crêpes à la florentine

serves 4

8 ready-made crêpes

800g (1lb 12oz) frozen spinach

8 tbsp breadcrumbs

8 tbsp grated parmesan

8 eggs

salt and pepper

1 Pre-heat the grill to medium.

2 Fold the pancakes into quarters and place in a large ovenproof dish.

3 In a small pan cook the spinach in its own moisture for 4-5 minutes until it is hot. Drain well and spoon the spinach over the pancakes.

4 Sprinkle the breadcrumbs and the parmesan on top of the spinach and pancakes. Place under the grill for 5-6 minutes until the cheese is golden.

5 Meanwhile, place the eggs in a small pan of cold water and bring to the boil. Cook for 3 minutes so that the whites are set but the yolks still slightly runny. Then drain off the hot water and peel the shells from the eggs under cold running water. Then cut the eggs in half.

Serve the eggs on top of the pancakes so the egg yolk drizzles on to them.

Tip If you prefer a more traditional florentine, fry or poach the eggs. Make sure the yolks are fairly runny.

cheese, herb & bean feast pancakes

30 mins

serves 4

4 crespolini or other thick
ready-made pancakes

100g (3½oz) mozzarella
cheese, grated

100g (3½oz) cheddar cheese,
grated

1 tbsp fresh chopped parsley

1 tbsp fresh chopped oregano

400g can mixed beans,
drained

400g can red kidney beans,
drained

1 tbsp olive oil

1 garlic clove, crushed

1 onion, finely chopped

salt and pepper

4 ripe tomatoes, chopped

fresh basil leaves to garnish

1 Pre-heat the oven to
220°C/400°F/gas 6.
2 Heat the olive oil in a frying-
pan, add the garlic and onion
and fry for 3 minutes until
softened.
3 Stir in the herbs and beans
and season well. Cook for a
further 5 minutes. Scatter in
the mozzarella and cheddar,
stir well and remove the pan
from the heat.
4 Spoon the bean mixture
into the centre of each
pancake and then roll them
up. Put the pancakes in a large
ovenproof dish, scatter the
chopped tomatoes over the
top and place in the oven for
15-20 minutes.
Serve garnished with fresh
basil leaves.

25 mins

leeks with red wine, coriander & mint

serves 4

12 baby leeks, trimmed

100ml (3½fl oz) fruity red wine

1 tbsp coriander seeds, lightly crushed

2 tbsp roughly chopped fresh mint

1 tsp black peppercorns, lightly crushed

100ml (3½fl oz) olive oil

3 bay leaves

5-6 sprigs of thyme

1 tbsp honey

1 tbsp balsamic or sherry vinegar

salt

1 Place the coriander seeds and peppercorns in a large frying-pan. Dry fry over a medium heat for 2-3 minutes until the spices begin to release their fragrance. Then add the oil, bay leaves, thyme, honey, wine and vinegar. Stir to blend.

2 Add the leeks and bring the liquid to the boil, cover and simmer for 5 minutes. Uncover and cook for another 5-10 minutes until the leeks are just tender when tested with the tip of a sharp knife.

3 Transfer the leeks to a serving dish with a slotted spoon. If there is still a lot of liquid, boil it rapidly until there are only 4-5 tbsp left. Add salt to taste and pour over the leeks. Leave to cool.

Serve with the mint scattered over the leeks.

30 mins

couscous-stuffed peppers

serves 4

225g (8oz) couscous

4 yellow or red peppers, halved and deseeded

2 red onions

2 small courgettes

2 tomatoes

3 tbsp olive oil

55g (2oz) pinenuts

a few fresh basil leaves

salt and black pepper

1 Pre-heat the oven to 200°C/400°F/gas 6. Brush the peppers with 1 tbsp oil and roast for 10-15 minutes or until they soften and colour.
2 Meanwhile, soak the couscous in 425ml (15fl oz) boiling water for 5 minutes. Dice the onions and courgettes. Deseed and dice the tomatoes.
3 Heat 2 tbsp oil and fry the onion for 5 minutes until soft. Add the courgettes and pinenuts and cook for 5 minutes. Add the tomatoes and cook for a further minute until they begin to soften.
4 Tear the basil leaves and stir, with the vegetables, into the couscous; season to taste.
Serve the couscous piled into the roasted pepper halves.

stuffed aubergine gratin

30 mins

serves 4

4 aubergines, halved

115g (4oz) rice

2 tbsp olive oil

1 onion, finely sliced

115g (4oz) button mushrooms, halved

2 garlic cloves, crushed

200g (7oz) can plum tomatoes, drained

1 green pepper, chopped

4 tbsp chopped fresh parsley

115g (4oz) cheddar, grated

1 Pre-heat the oven to 200°C/400°F/gas 6. Prick the aubergines with a fork, place on an oiled baking sheet and roast for 25 minutes, until tender when pricked with the point of a knife.

2 Meanwhile cook the rice in a large pan of boiling water. Drain, refresh and set aside.

3 Heat the oil in a large frying-pan and fry the onion, mushrooms and garlic until softened. Add the rice and tomatoes and season to taste. Bring to the boil and simmer for 5 minutes.

4 Scoop out the aubergine flesh. Mix it with the rice and tomato mixture, pepper and parsley. Spoon back into the aubergine skins and scatter the cheese over the top. Place under the hot grill for 2 minutes until the cheese melts and is bubbling.

Serve with a crunchy salad of green peppers and celery.

hot and spicy

chicken, coconut & spinach curry

30 mins

serves 4

500g (1lb 2oz) chicken, boneless thighs or breasts, cut into 5cm (2in) pieces

400ml (14fl oz) can coconut milk

115g (4oz) fresh spinach leaves, washed and trimmed

2 tbsp oil

2 onions, finely chopped

2 garlic cloves, chopped

3 green chillies, deseeded and finely sliced

2 tsp ground coriander

6 cardamom pods, lightly crushed

3 fresh bay leaves

salt and pepper

2 large tomatoes, chopped

1 tbsp chopped fresh coriander

juice of 1 lemon

1 Heat the oil in a pan and fry half the onion for 5 minutes. Add the garlic, two thirds of the chillies, ground coriander and cardamom and cook for 2 minutes.

2 Add the chicken and coat well. Brown for 2-3 minutes.

3 Add the coconut milk and bay leaves and simmer for 15 minutes. Taste and season.

4 Meanwhile, for the relish, mix the rest of the onion, chilli and the tomato in a bowl. Add the coriander and lemon juice.

5 Add the spinach to the chicken and cook for 3-4 minutes until it wilts. Remove the bay leaves.

Serve with the relish.

25 mins

chunky chicken & vegetable balti

serves 4

4 large chicken legs, skinned, boned and cubed

6 tbsp medium Balti curry paste

2 tbsp sunflower oil

2 onions, sliced

2 green peppers, deseeded and sliced

55g (2oz) mushrooms, sliced

175g (6oz) broccoli florets, blanched

175g (6oz) cauliflower florets, blanched

naan breads to serve

1 Heat the oil in a saucepan and stir-fry the chicken in 2 batches for 5 minutes each until golden. Remove with a slotted spoon and set aside.
2 Add onions, peppers and mushrooms to the pan and cook for 5 minutes until soft. Add the curry paste, 150ml (5fl oz) water and chicken and bring to the boil. Cover and simmer for 10 minutes.
3 Remove the lid and add the broccoli and cauliflower and cook until warmed through.
Serve with plenty of warmed naan breads.

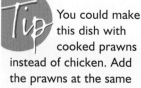

Tip You could make this dish with cooked prawns instead of chicken. Add the prawns at the same time as the cauliflower and broccoli florets.

30 mins

aromatic chicken-topped naan

serves 2

2 skinless, boneless chicken breasts, cut into chunks

2 naan breads

250g (9oz) natural yoghurt

1 tsp ground cinnamon

1 tsp ground ginger

2 tsp ground cumin

2 tbsp mango chutney

4 tsp vegetable oil

1 red pepper, deseeded and sliced

2 tbsp lemon juice

2 tbsp chopped fresh coriander

knob of butter, melted

fresh coriander, to garnish

1 Make the marinade by mixing 200g (7oz) yoghurt with the spices and chutney in a non-metallic bowl. Add the chicken and mix well. Set aside for at least 10 minutes – longer if possible.

2 Meanwhile, heat the naan bread according to packet instructions. Heat half the oil in a frying-pan and cook the red pepper for 5 minutes, until slightly softened.

3 Heat the remaining oil in a separate frying-pan and stir-fry the chicken for 5 minutes, until cooked through.

4 Make the dressing by mixing the remaining yoghurt with the lemon juice and chopped coriander. Brush butter over the naans. Divide the chicken and pepper between the naans. **Serve** drizzled with the yoghurt dressing and garnished with the fresh coriander.

diced chicken in black bean sauce

20 mins

serves 4

4 chicken breasts, diced

2 tbsp black bean paste

1½ tsp salt

1 egg white, lightly beaten

2 tsp cornflour, mixed to a paste with a little water

3-4 tbsp vegetable oil

2.5cm (1in) piece root ginger, peeled and chopped

3 spring onions, chopped

225g (8oz) can bamboo shoots, drained and sliced

1 tsp caster sugar

1 tbsp soy sauce

2 tbsp sake (Japanese rice spirit) or dry sherry

1 red chilli, deseeded and sliced

1 Mix the salt, egg white and cornflour paste in a large bowl. Add the chicken pieces and stir well to coat them thoroughly.
2 Heat a large wok or frying-pan and add 2 tbsp oil. Once the oil starts to smoke, add the chicken. Stir-fry for 5-10 minutes, turning until cooked through. Remove from the pan using a slotted spoon and set aside for a few minutes.
3 Re-heat the pan or wok and pour in 2 tbsp oil. Fry the ginger and onions until softened. Add the bamboo shoots, sugar, soy sauce, sake or sherry, black bean paste and chilli and stir-fry briefly.
4 Return the chicken to the pan and stir-fry until it is well coated with sauce and hot.
Serve with boiled rice or noodles.

spicy chicken on fruity couscous

30 mins

serves 4

4 skinless, boneless chicken breasts

3 tbsp olive oil

pinch of cayenne

2 tbsp chopped fresh coriander

2 tbsp chopped fresh parsley

½ tsp ground coriander

½ tsp ground cumin

1 tsp paprika

1 garlic clove, crushed

juice of 1 lemon

salt and black pepper

175g (6oz) couscous

25g (1oz) ready-to-eat dried peaches, finely chopped

175g (6oz) tomatoes, chopped

25g (1oz) raisins

fresh coriander, to garnish

1 Mix 2 tbsp oil with the cayenne, 1 tbsp fresh coriander, the fresh parsley, spices, garlic and lemon juice; season to taste.

2 Cut slashes in the chicken and coat with the herb and spice mix. Cover and set aside for as long as possible.

3 Pour 300ml (10fl oz) boiling water on the couscous and set aside for 5 minutes. Then stir in the peaches, tomatoes, raisins and remaining coriander and oil. Season and set aside.

4 Grill the chicken under a moderate grill for 3-4 minutes on each side, until the chicken is cooked through.

Serve the chicken sliced, on top of the couscous and garnished with fresh coriander.

turkey patties & bruschetta

30 mins

serves 4

500g (1lb 2oz) minced turkey

8 slices French bread

4 tbsp olive oil

1 large green chilli, deseeded and finely chopped

2 large garlic cloves, crushed

large pinch of ground cumin

salt and black pepper

2 large tomatoes, halved

4 large field mushrooms

4 large fresh basil leaves, shredded, to garnish

relish or mustard, to serve

1 Heat 1 tbsp oil in a small pan and cook the chilli and garlic for 1-2 minutes until soft. Add the cumin and cook for a few seconds; leave to cool.

2 Stir the chilli and garlic into the minced turkey and season to taste. Divide the mixture into 4 and shape into patties.

3 Heat 1 tbsp oil in a frying-pan over moderate heat and fry the patties for 4-5 minutes, turning once. Remove from the pan with a slotted spoon and keep warm.

4 Heat the grill to high. Put 1 tbsp oil in the frying-pan and fry the mushrooms and tomatoes for 3-4 minutes, turning once.

5 Meanwhile, make the bruschetta: toast the bread on both sides and then brush with the remaining oil. Divide the bruschetta, mushrooms, tomatoes and patties between 4 serving plates.

Serve sprinkled with the basil and accompanied by a relish or mustard.

20 mins

thai lamb curry with noodles

serves 4

4 lamb steaks, chopped

4 tbsp Thai red curry paste

225g (8oz) rice noodles

1 tbsp sunflower oil

115g (4oz) shiitake or button mushrooms, sliced

225g (8oz) butternut squash, peeled, deseeded and cut into cubes

2 x 400ml (14fl oz) cans coconut milk

2 tbsp tomato purée

6 tbsp light soy sauce

115g (4oz) sugar snap peas, shredded

1 red pepper, finely sliced

bunch of fresh coriander

bunch of fresh basil

1 Place the rice noodles in a bowl and pour boiling water over. Leave to soak for a few minutes until softened.

2 Heat the oil in a wok or large frying-pan and add the lamb and mushrooms. Stir-fry for 3-4 minutes. Add the squash and stir-fry for a further minute.

3 Stir in the coconut milk, the curry paste, tomato purée and soy sauce. Leave to simmer for 5 minutes.

4 Stir in the sugar snaps and red pepper and cook for a further 5 minutes. Add most of the coriander and basil. Drain the noodles, add to the pan and toss well.

Serve the curry garnished with the remaining coriander and basil.

oriental-style sticky lamb chops

25 mins

serves 4

8 chump lamb chops
320g (11oz) jar plum sauce
4 tsp clear honey
4 tsp dark soy sauce
2 garlic cloves, crushed
2.5cm (1in) ginger, chopped
2 spring onions, cut into
2.5cm (1in) long pieces
2 red chillies, finely chopped
250g (9oz) pkt egg noodles
1 tbsp sesame oil
3 spring onions for curling
227g (8oz) can water
chestnuts, drained and roughly
chopped
227g (8oz) can bamboo
shoots, drained
1 red chilli, finely sliced

1 Pre-heat the oven 220°C/425°F/gas 7.
2 Mix half the plum sauce with honey, soy sauce, garlic, ginger, spring onion and half the chopped chillies.
3 Place the chops in a roasting tin and coat with the sauce. Marinate for 3-4 minutes.
4 Roast in the oven for 12-15 minutes, turning once.
5 Drop noodles into boiling water and cook until tender. Then toss them in sesame oil with spring onion curls, water chestnuts and bamboo shoots.
Serve the lamb on the noodles with sauce spooned over the top. Garnish with chilli slices.

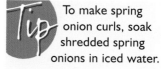

Tip To make spring onion curls, soak shredded spring onions in iced water.

20 mins

mexican lamb tortillas

serves 4

450g (1lb) minced lamb

4 ready-made tortillas

1 onion, finely chopped

1 garlic clove, crushed

1 egg beaten

2 tbsp olive oil

2 ripe avocados

juice of 1 lemon

1 large red onion, chopped

2 red peppers, chopped

2 firm tomatoes, chopped

1 tsp chopped parsley

parsley to garnish

1 Pre-heat the oven to 190°C/375°F/gas 5. Mix the lamb with the finely chopped onion and garlic. Add the egg and mix well. Heat the oil in a frying-pan. Divide the mixture into 16 and roll into balls.

2 Fry the balls for 6-7 minutes until browned on the outside and cooked on the inside. Place the tortillas in the oven to warm through.

3 Scoop the avocado flesh out of the shells and mash roughly using a fork. Add the lemon juice and mix in.

4 Place a tortilla shell on each plate and divide the red onion, pepper, tomatoes and chopped parsley between them. Spoon the avocado mixture on top of the salad. **Serve** the meatballs on top of the salad and garnish with flatleaf parsley.

Tip For a Tex-Mex flavour, grate some mature cheddar on top.

spicy beefy meatball stew

30 mins

serves 4

450g (1lb) minced beef

2 onions, finely chopped

4 garlic cloves, crushed

2 green chillies, deseeded and finely chopped

55g (2oz) can green pitted olives, half roughly chopped

salt and pepper

1 egg, beaten

2 courgettes, thickly sliced

1 small aubergine, chopped

150ml (5fl oz) chicken or beef stock

200g (7oz) can chopped tomatoes

2 tbsp tomato purée

Tabasco sauce

1 Mix the beef, half the onions, garlic and chillies together. Add the chopped olives and season well. Mix the egg in thoroughly.
2 Divide the mixture into 20 balls. Heat the oil in a large frying-pan and add the rest of the onions. Fry until softened then add the meatballs.
3 Cook for 5-6 minutes until brown on the outside and cooked on the inside. Add the courgettes and aubergine and cook for a further 2-3 minutes.
4 Add the stock, chopped tomatoes and tomato purée and a few drops of Tabasco sauce. Turn the heat up high and boil until the sauce is reduced and thickened.
5 Add the remaining olives and adjust the seasoning. Cook for 2 more minutes. **Serve** with warm crusty bread.

barbecued beef with black bean sauce

25 mins

serves 4

450g (1lb) sirloin steak or fillet of beef

85g (3oz) shiitake or other small mushrooms

1 red pepper, deseeded and cut into large pieces

5 tbsp black bean sauce

4 tbsp light soy sauce

3 tbsp light brown sugar

1 tbsp olive oil

1 Cut the beef into four even pieces. Place each piece between two sheets of plastic film and bat out to a thickness of 5mm (¼in). Cut into strips and thread on to four skewers alternating with the mushrooms and red pepper.
2 Mix the remaining ingredients together and spoon over the beef and vegetables on the skewers, covering them evenly. Leave to marinate for 10 minutes.
3 Grill or barbecue the skewers for 4-5 minutes, turning occasionally.
Serve with egg noodles sprinkled with toasted sesame seeds and a little chopped spring onion.

Tip Batting out the meat makes it quick and easy to cook. Use a rolling pin, meat hammer or the flat side of a cleaver.

beef with lemon grass & basil

15 mins

serves 4

600g (1lb 5oz) sirloin steak, finely sliced

2 stalks lemon grass, finely chopped

2 tbsp shredded basil

1 tbsp sunflower oil

4 shallots, chopped

2 green chillies, chopped

2 tsp brown sugar

juice of 1 lemon

1 papaya, peeled, deseeded and sliced

salt and pepper

1 Heat the oil in a wok or deep frying-pan. Add the lemon grass, shallots and chillies, and stir-fry for 2 minutes.

2 Add the beef and stir-fry for about 5 minutes until cooked through. Stir in the sugar, lemon juice and papaya.

3 Stir-fry for a further minute until warmed through. Mix in half the basil. Season to taste. **Serve** with steamed jasmine rice. Garnish with the rest of the chopped basil.

Tip When preparing lemon grass, only use the pale, soft, lower half of the stalks.

30 mins

pork chops with orange & soy

serves 4

4 pork chops

zest and juice of 1 orange

2 tbsp soy sauce

1 tbsp brown sugar

2 crumbled cinnamon sticks

2 star anise

2 tbsp olive oil

1 packet stir-fry vegetables

orange zest strips to garnish

1 Pre-heat the grill to high. Put the orange juice and zest in a pan with the soy sauce, brown sugar, cinnamon, and star anise. Bring to the boil and reduce the liquid by half.

2 Cool and strain the sauce. Brush the sauce over the pork chops and grill for 4-5 minutes on either side, basting continuously. Leave the pork chops to rest for 5 minutes once they are cooked.

3 Meanwhile, heat the oil in a large frying-pan and add the vegetables. Stir-fry for 4-5 minutes over a high heat.

Serve the pork chops on top of the vegetables and drizzle the pan juices over. Garnish with strips of orange zest.

Tip For a mixture of eastern and western traditions, use pure unsweetened apple juice instead of the orange juice to make the sauce. Garnish with apple slices or a little lemon zest.

gingered pork on watercress

30 mins

serves 4

500g (1lb 2oz) pork fillet, sliced

3 tsp minced ginger

500g (1lb 2oz) waxy potatoes, scrubbed and cut into 1cm (½in) slices

salt and pepper

4 tsp sesame seeds

2 eggs, beaten

1 tbsp sesame oil

2 tbsp vegetable oil

1 tsp cornflour

3 tbsp dry sherry

1 tbsp soy sauce

bunch of watercress, rinsed

1 Mix the pork and ginger and set aside.

2 Boil the potatoes in lightly salted water for 10-12 minutes until tender, then drain.

3 Dry-fry the sesame seeds in a frying-pan until lightly toasted, then leave to cool.

4 Season eggs and mix in the sesame seeds. Heat sesame oil and 1 tsp vegetable oil in a frying-pan. Swirl egg round the pan to make a thin omelette. When cooled, cut into strips.

5 Heat remaining oil in frying-pan and fry the pork for 1-2 minutes on each side. Transfer to a plate.

6 Mix cornflour with 2 tbsp water, stir into the sherry and soy sauce, then pour into the pan. Stir until it thickens. Return pork to the pan to heat through. **Serve** the pork on the watercress and potatoes, topped with the sauce and omelette strips.

30 mins

chunky chilli pork tortillas

serves 4

450g (1lb) pork fillet or boned loin, cut into thin strips

8 flour tortillas

1 small red chilli, deseeded and chopped

1 tsp ground coriander

1 garlic clove, crushed

4 tbsp lime juice

2 tbsp sunflower oil

75g (3oz) onion, thinly sliced

400g (14oz) can red kidney beans, rinsed and drained

150g (5oz) beef tomatoes, skinned, deseeded and diced

salt and black pepper

4 tbsp natural yoghurt

2 tbsp chopped fresh mint

2 limes, cut into wedges, to serve

1 Put the pork in a bowl and mix with the chilli, coriander, garlic and lime juice to coat evenly. Leave to marinate for 10 minutes – longer if possible.
2 Heat the oil in a frying-pan and fry the onion for 3-4 minutes until it browns. Add the pork and cook for 10 minutes until the meat is browned, stirring frequently.
3 Add the kidney beans and tomatoes and season well. Simmer for 3-4 minutes until the tomatoes have softened.
4 Warm the tortillas under the grill for about 1 minute, turning once. Divide the pork mixture between the tortillas and top with the yoghurt and mint. Fold up the tortillas.
Serve with the lime wedges.

25 mins

spicy sausage & cheese grill

serves 4

6 spicy sausages

200g (7oz) ricotta cheese, crumbled

55g (2oz) pecorino cheese, grated

2 tbsp olive oil

2 small red onions, chopped

2 red peppers, chopped

1 chorizo sausage, sliced

salt and pepper

150ml (5fl oz) barbecue sauce, home-made or from a jar or packet

200g (7oz) can chopped tomatoes

40g (1½oz) fresh breadcrumbs

2 tbsp fresh chopped basil

1 Grill the spicy sausages for 12 minutes until they are cooked through and browned. Cut into bite-sized pieces.
2 Meanwhile heat the oil in a frying-pan and add the onions and peppers. Fry for 2-3 minutes until softened. Pre-heat the grill to high.
3 Add the chorizo sausage and season. Mix in the barbecue sauce and chopped tomatoes and simmer for a further 5 minutes. Stir in the sausages and make sure they are heated through.
4 Place in a dish and scatter the ricotta, pecorino, breadcrumbs and half the basil on top. Grill for 3 minutes.
Serve with the rest of the basil sprinkled on top.

20 mins

cod & green pepper masala

serves 4

675g (1½lb) chunky cod fillet, skinned and cut into 7.5cm (3in) cubes

1 green pepper, deseeded and cut into large pieces

2 tbsp oil

225g (8oz) onion, thinly sliced

250g (9oz) white long-grain rice

350g (12oz) jar green lime masala sauce

100ml (4fl oz) fish stock or water

juice of 1 lime

1 bunch fresh mint, roughly chopped

lime wedges to serve

1 Heat the oil in a large frying-pan or wok and add the onion and pepper. Fry gently for 8-10 minutes.
2 Add the rice to a large pan of boiling salted water, cook for 12 minutes, drain, then rinse in hot water.
3 Add the masala sauce, stock or water and lime juice to the frying-pan. Heat through, then add the fish and simmer for 5 minutes or until the fish is opaque. Stir in the chopped mint.
Serve immediately with the rice and lime wedges.

Tip If you can't find green lime masala sauce, you can use any jar of masala sauce instead.

spicy smoked haddock kedgeree

25 mins

serves 4

2 eggs

350g (12oz) skinless smoked haddock

280g (10oz) basmati rice

25g (1oz) butter

1 onion, finely chopped

2 tbsp grated fresh ginger

1 tbsp Madras curry paste

1 red chilli, thinly sliced

200ml (7fl oz) milk

4 tbsp Greek yoghurt

4 tbsp finely chopped fresh parsley

55g (2oz) toasted almonds

poppadums to serve

mango chutney to serve

1 Boil the eggs for 10 minutes. In another pan, boil the rice for 10-15 minutes, until tender. Drain the rice. Peel and quarter the eggs.

2 Meanwhile, melt the butter in a frying-pan and add the onion and ginger. Fry for 3-4 minutes until softened. Stir in the curry paste and chilli and cook for a further 3 minutes. Transfer to a large bowl.

3 Pour the milk into the empty frying-pan, warm to a simmer and add the haddock. Poach for 5 minutes until almost cooked. Remove the haddock from the pan and flake into the bowl containing the spicy onions.

4 Toss in the rice and yoghurt and stir until well coated. Add the parsley and almonds. Top the dish off with the eggs.
Serve with poppadums and mango chutney.

oriental seared tuna

30 mins

serves 4

4 tuna steaks

1 tbsp soy sauce

2 sliced spring onions

1 small red chilli, deseeded and chopped

2.5cm (1in) piece fresh root ginger, peeled and grated

juice and zest of 1 lime

1 tbsp olive oil

250g (9oz) packet egg noodles

250g (9oz) packet ready-prepared stir-fry vegetables

chopped fresh coriander, to garnish

1 Mix the soy sauce, spring onions, chilli, ginger and lime juice and zest in a shallow, non-metallic bowl.

2 Turn the tuna in the marinade to coat completely. Set aside for 20 minutes, or longer if possible.

3 Brush a griddle pan with the oil and put over high heat. Take the tuna out of the marinade and pat dry; reserve the marinade. Cook the tuna for 2-3 minutes on each side. Turn the tuna around during cooking if you want to achieve a criss-cross effect.

4 Meanwhile, cook the noodles in boiling water, according to packet instructions, and stir-fry the vegetables.

Serve the tuna on the noodles and vegetables, drizzled with the remaining marinade and garnished with fresh coriander.

thai spiced salmon with noodles

30 mins

serves 4

4 salmon fillets

2 tsp Thai 7-spice seasoning

250g (9oz) packet egg noodles

2 tbsp olive oil

1 tbsp light soy sauce

1 cucumber, peeled

2 tbsp rice vinegar

2 tsp caster sugar

1 tbsp sesame oil

2 tbsp sesame seeds, toasted

coriander leaves for garnish

1 Mix together the Thai 7-spice seasoning, olive oil and soy sauce. Put the salmon into an ovenproof dish and pour over the spice mixture. Cover and leave to marinate for 5 minutes.

2 Meanwhile, peel long ribbons from the cucumber with a potato peeler. Mix the rice vinegar and sugar. When the sugar has dissolved, pour the dressing over the cucumber and mix together well. Set aside.

3 Cook the noodles according to the packet instructions. When cooked, drain and toss with the sesame oil and sesame seeds.

4 Grill the salmon for 8-10 minutes until cooked and the skin is crispy, basting frequently to keep the fish moist.

Serve the salmon on top of the noodles with the cucumber ribbons on the side. Garnish with a few coriander leaves.

coriander fish cakes with dipping sauce

30 mins

serves 4

6 tbsp chopped fresh coriander

225g (8oz) cod fillet, skinned and boned

225g (8oz) salmon fillet, skinned and boned

600g (1lb 5oz) floury potatoes – Maris Piper are good

2 tbsp olive oil

salt and pepper

100ml (3½fl oz) rice vinegar

2 tsp sugar

2 red chillies, deseeded and chopped

bunch spring onions, chopped

2 tbsp fish sauce

4 tbsp flour, seasoned

2 tbsp sunflower oil

1 Pre-heat oven to 200°C/400°F/gas 6.
2 Boil the potatoes until tender; drain and mash well.
3 Put the cod and salmon into a roasting tin, drizzle over the oil and sprinkle with pepper. Roast for 10 minutes. When cooled slightly, flake coarsely into a bowl.
4 To make the dipping sauce, mix the vinegar, sugar, chillies and 2 tbsp coriander together.
5 Lightly fold the fish, spring onions, the fish sauce and the rest of the coriander into the mashed potato and season.
6 Shape the mixture into 12 patties. Coat in seasoned flour. Heat the oil in a frying-pan. Fry the fish cakes for 2-3 minutes on each side until golden.
Serve with a salad and the dipping sauce on the side.

barbecued jumbo prawns

30 mins

serves 4

36 raw jumbo prawns

425ml (15fl oz) sake

2 tbsp tamarind concentrate

6 tbsp dry sherry

125ml (4fl oz) light soy sauce

115g (4oz) light soft brown sugar

2 tbsp finely chopped ginger

2 tbsp finely chopped shallot

4 garlic cloves, crushed

2 tbsp tomato ketchup

2 red chillies, deseeded and finely chopped

1 In a heavy-based saucepan, mix together and heat all the ingredients except the prawns.
2 Simmer for 15 minutes, until reduced by about a half. Then remove from the heat and allow to cool.
3 Thread the prawns on to 12 wooden skewers that have been soaked in water. Pour half the marinade over the prawns and leave to marinate for 10 minutes.
4 Barbecue the prawns for about 2 minutes on each side, basting frequently.
Serve immediately, with the rest of the marinade in a dipping bowl on the side.

Tip If you can't find sake, which is Japanese rice wine, then use dry sherry instead. Similarly, use 1 tbsp of lemon juice mixed with a little Worcestershire sauce if you cannot get hold of tamarind concentrate.

30 mins

king prawn kebabs on coconut rice

serves 4

450g (1lb) fresh king prawns

350g (12oz) basmati rice

small pinch of saffron strands

1 stick fresh lemon grass, bruised and roughly chopped

150ml (5fl oz) coconut milk

450g (1lb) haddock, cut into large pieces

4-8 small ripe plum tomatoes

1 green pepper, deseeded and cut into pieces

1 red pepper, deseeded and cut into pieces

1 large onion, cut in wedges

2 tbsp lemon juice

3 tbsp basil-flavoured olive oil

salt and pepper

1 Bring a large pan of salted water to the boil. Add the rice, saffron and lemon grass and cook for 5 minutes. Then add the coconut milk and cook for a further 5 minutes. Drain and remove the lemon grass. Pre-heat the grill to high.
2 Meanwhile, peel the prawns, leaving the tails intact, and remove the black vein from the back of each. Thread the prawns, fish and vegetables on to 4 skewers and lay in the base of a shallow dish.
3 Stir the lemon juice and olive oil together and drizzle over the kebabs. Season and leave to marinate for 5 minutes.
4 Grill the kebabs for 8-10 minutes until the haddock is opaque and cooked through.
Serve one kebab per portion, laying each one on a bed of coconut rice.

curried prawns with pitta bread

25 mins

serves 4

350g (12oz) frozen peeled tiger prawns, thawed

4 pitta breads

3 tbsp olive oil

2 large garlic cloves, crushed

1 tsp paprika

1 tsp ground cumin

½ tsp ground ginger

bunch of fresh coriander, chopped

25g (1oz) pinenuts

50g (2oz) packet rocket leaves

75g (3oz) packet watercress

1 medium onion, thinly sliced

4 tbsp natural yoghurt

1 lemon, quartered

salt and pepper

1 Place the pitta breads in a low oven to warm.

2 Heat the oil in a wok or frying-pan and add the garlic and spices. Stir over a low heat for 1 minute.

3 Increase the heat to high and add the prawns. Stir-fry for 2 minutes or until they turn pink. Add the coriander and cook for another 30 seconds. Season, then mix in the pinenuts.

4 Take the pitta breads from the oven, tear them in half and place one on each plate. Divide the rocket, watercress and onion slices between the plates. Spoon the prawns and their juices on to the leaves.

Serve with a generous dollop of yoghurt and a squeeze of lemon juice over the prawns.

25 mins

oriental prawn spring rolls

serves 4

8 sheets ready-made spring roll pastry

vegetable oil for deep-frying

400g (14oz) prawns, chopped

2 red peppers, chopped

100g (3½oz) water chestnuts, chopped

2 spring onions, chopped

100g (3½oz) bean sprouts

100g (3½oz) cooked noodles

2 tsp five-spice powder

2 tsp soy sauce

salt and pepper

chilli dipping sauce to serve

1 Heat the oil in a deep saucepan or in a deep fat fryer.
2 Mix the prawns, peppers, water chestnuts, spring onions, bean sprouts and noodles together in a bowl.
3 Add the five-spice powder and soy sauce, season and mix thoroughly until all the ingredients are coated.
4 Place 2 tbsp of the mixture in a corner of one sheet of pastry. Roll diagonally, pulling in the corners.
5 Deep fry the spring rolls in two batches for 4-5 minutes until golden and crisp.
Serve the spring rolls with chilli dipping sauce.

Tip Make your own chilli dipping sauce by mixing chilli oil, a finely sliced red chilli and a dash of vinegar.

spicy prawn stir-fry with rice

15 mins

serves 4

20 fresh king prawns, peeled, tails left on

400g (14oz) easy-cook rice

2 tbsp sesame oil

2 small onions, chopped

4 garlic cloves, crushed

8 red chillies, halved lengthways

1 red pepper, chopped

1 green pepper, chopped

4 celery sticks, chopped

55g (2oz) dried mushrooms, soaked in boiling water

salt and pepper

1 tsp chilli oil

1 tsp light soy sauce

1 tsp caraway seeds

1 tsp chopped fresh parsley

1 Bring a large pan of salted water to the boil and add the rice. Boil for 10-12 minutes; drain. Refresh under running water and set aside.

2 Meanwhile, heat a wok or large frying-pan and add the sesame oil. Continue to heat until the oil is hot.

3 Add the onion and garlic and fry until softened. Tip in the chillies, red pepper, green pepper, celery and mushrooms. Season and stir-fry for another 4-5 minutes.

4 Add the prawns to the frying-pan and stir-fry for 2 minutes then add the chilli oil, soy sauce and caraway seeds. Turn the heat up high to reduce the liquid for 1 minute.

5 Add the rice and parsley and toss well in the pan.

Serve with a little soy sauce on the side.

spicy prawn flaky pie

30 mins

serves 4

400g (14oz) packet filo pastry

280g (10oz) cooked king prawns

300ml (10fl oz) milk

1 onion, quartered

6 black peppercorns

1 bay leaf

salt and pepper

55g (2oz) butter

25g (1oz) plain flour

1 tbsp English mustard

2 tsp cayenne pepper

200g (7oz) can artichoke hearts, drained

1 tbsp chopped fresh parsley

1 Pre-heat the oven to 200°C/400°F/gas 6. Heat the milk in a small saucepan and add the onion quarters, peppercorns and bay leaf. Season slightly and bring to a gentle simmer. Strain the milk and put to one side.

2 Melt half the butter in a saucepan and add the flour. Stir to a thick paste then gradually add the milk, stirring all the time to form a thick white sauce. Add the mustard and cayenne pepper.

3 Add the artichoke hearts and prawns to the sauce and season well. Place the mixture in a pie dish.

4 Melt the remaining butter and brush the pastry sheets with it. Layer the sheets on top of the pie dish.

5 Bake the pie for 15 minutes until the pastry is golden.

Serve garnished with coriander or parsley.

quick & easy gumbo

30 mins

serves 4

1 tbsp oil

25g (1oz) butter

1 onion, sliced

1 small green pepper, deseeded and chopped

2 celery sticks, chopped

2 tbsp plain flour

300ml (10fl oz) fish or vegetable stock

300g (10oz) fresh okra, trimmed

400g (14oz) can chopped tomatoes

1 bay leaf

½ tsp cayenne pepper

1 tsp paprika

200g (7oz) kabanos or smoked frankfurters

170g (6oz) can crabmeat, drained

250g (9oz) can smoked or unsmoked mussels, drained

1 Heat the oil and butter in a large pan and cook the onion for 5 minutes until soft. Add the pepper and celery and cook for a few minutes.
2 Sprinkle on the flour and mix well. Cook for 2 minutes.
3 Gradually stir in the stock and add the okra, tomatoes, bay leaf, cayenne and paprika; simmer for 15 minutes.
4 Chop the sausage into 1cm (½in) pieces and add to the pan. Add the crabmeat and mussels. Continue cooking for 2-3 minutes until completely heated through.
Serve in bowls accompanied by plain boiled long-grain rice.

20 mins

crisp onion bhajis

serves 4

450g (1lb) onions, thinly sliced

1 tsp ground cumin

2 tsp ground coriander

1 tbsp chopped fresh coriander

1 tsp coriander seeds, crushed

1 tsp salt

1 green chilli, chopped

175g (6oz) gram flour

sunflower oil for deep-frying

chopped fresh coriander and lemon wedges to serve

1 Place the spices, salt, fresh coriander and chilli in a bowl and stir well.

2 Sift the gram flour into the spicy herb mixture in the bowl and mix with 8-10 tbsp water to make a thick paste. Then add the onions.

3 Heat the oil in a deep saucepan or deep-fat fryer. Drop in the onion mixture, a few spoonfuls at a time, and cook for 4 minutes, turning once, until crisp and golden.

4 Remove the bhajis from the pan with a slotted spoon and drain on kitchen paper. Repeat until all the mixture is used up.

Serve garnished with fresh coriander and lemon wedges.

Tip Gram flour (besan) is made from chickpeas. It's available from Indian shops and supermarkets.

potato & green bean curry

30 mins

serves 4

500g (1lb 2oz) small new potatoes

250g (9oz) fine green beans, topped and tailed, cut in 2.5cm (1in) lengths

25g (1oz) butter

3 tbsp sunflower oil

2 small green chillies

1 tsp cumin seeds

1 tsp ground turmeric

1 garlic clove, crushed

salt

½ tsp garam masala

1 Scrub the new potatoes and cut them in half.

2 Heat the butter and oil in a wide shallow saucepan and turn up the heat. When the fat is sizzling, stir in the whole green chillies, cumin seeds and turmeric.

3 Add the garlic and fry for 30 seconds. Add the potatoes and season with salt. Stir until coated with the spiced butter and oil.

4 Stir in the beans, cover the pan and reduce the heat to moderate. Cook for 10 minutes, stirring occasionally. Add the garam masala and cook for another 5 minutes.

Serve as soon as the potatoes are tender.

25 mins

curried scrambled eggs

serves 4

12 eggs, beaten

1 tsp mild curry powder

55g (2oz) butter

1 large onion, finely chopped

1 garlic clove, crushed

2.5cm (1in) fresh ginger, grated

1 red chilli, finely chopped

pinch of salt

pinch of sugar (optional)

1 tbsp fresh coriander, chopped

1 Heat butter in a small frying-pan. Add onion, garlic, ginger and chilli and cook without colouring for 5 minutes.

2 Add curry powder to the pan and continue to cook for about 2 minutes.

3 Pour on the eggs and season with salt and the sugar, if using. (The sugar gives you a slightly sweeter curry flavour.)

4 Stir the eggs until they are softly scrambled.

Serve with warm naan bread or on slices of brown toast, and sprinkled with fresh coriander.

Tip A simple relish of chopped red onion mixed with chopped tomato eats very well with this dish.

indian chickpea & spinach patties

30 mins

serves 4

400g (14oz) can chickpeas, rinsed

115g (4oz) fresh spinach

3 garlic cloves, crushed

2 tsp grated root ginger

5cm (2in) cinnamon stick

4 cloves

2 tsp coriander seeds

2 tsp cumin seeds

½ tsp black peppercorns

1-2 green chillies, deseeded

8-10 fresh mint leaves

2 tbsp chopped fresh coriander

1 egg

55g (2oz) chopped onion

1 tbsp sunflower oil

1 Put the drained chickpeas in a pan with the washed spinach, garlic and ginger. Cook for 1-2 minutes, cover and continue cooking for 10-12 minutes, stirring occasionally.

2 Meanwhile, dry-fry the spices until they start to smell. Cool on a plate.

3 Grind the spices finely. Blitz in a food processor with the chickpea/spinach mixture, chillies, herbs, egg and salt to taste. Add the onion and pulse briefly.

4 Heat grill to high. Press the mixture into 8 round patties about 5cm (2in) in diameter.

5 Line a grill pan with foil and brush with oil. Brush patties with oil and grill for 4 minutes. Turn them over, brush with the remaining oil and grill for 3-4 minutes until brown and crisp.

Serve two patties on a grilled pitta bread, garnished with a sprig of mint.

20 mins

sweet chilli & cashew stir-fry

serves 4

4 tbsp sweet chilli dipping sauce

200g (7oz) cashew nuts, toasted

600g (1lb 5oz) noodles

2 tbsp sesame oil

2 garlic cloves, crushed

5cm (2in) piece ginger, peeled and finely sliced

250g (9oz) baby sweetcorn, halved lengthways

400g (14oz) sugar snap peas

1 orange pepper, finely sliced

200g (7oz) enoki mushrooms

salt and pepper

1 Bring a pan of water to the boil and cook the noodles according to the packet instructions. Drain and refresh the cooked noodles under cold water.

2 Heat a wok or large frying-pan until very hot and add the oil. Stir-fry the garlic and the ginger for a minute. Add the baby sweetcorn, peas, pepper and cashew nuts. Stir-fry for a further 3 minutes.

3 Add the noodles and the chilli sauce to the wok and stir-fry for a further 2 minutes. Stir in the mushrooms and stir-fry for 2 more minutes.

Serve immediately with plenty of seasoning.

20 mins

deep-fried sweet & sour tofu

serves 4

200g (7oz) tofu, cut into 2cm (¾in) cubes

oil for deep-frying

1 tsp groundnut oil

2 cucumbers, cut into large chunks

115g (4oz) unsalted roasted peanuts

2 tbsp sugar

3 tbsp light soy sauce

3 tbsp rice vinegar

1 tbsp tomato purée

1 tsp cornflour mixed with a little water to form a paste

rice or egg noodles to serve

1 Heat 2.5cm (1in) of the deep-frying oil in a wok or large frying-pan. When hot, add the tofu and deep-fry for 3 minutes, then set aside in a large bowl. Carefully drain off the oil from the pan.

2 Heat the groundnut oil in the wok or frying-pan. When it is hot, stir-fry the cucumber and peanuts for 3-4 minutes. Remove from the pan, leaving behind any juices, mix with the tofu and cover the bowl.

3 To make the sweet and sour sauce, add the sugar, soy sauce, rice vinegar and tomato purée to the wok or frying-pan. Stir well to blend all the ingredients together, then simmer gently for 1-2 minutes. Mix in the cornflour paste and stir until thickened. Spoon the sauce over the tofu, cucumber and peanuts. **Serve** with plain boiled rice or egg noodles.

25 mins

hot & spicy tex-mex platter

serves 4

420g (15oz) can mixed beans, drained

1 large ripe avocado, peeled and stoned

juice of ½ lime

284ml (10fl oz) tub soured cream

1 tsp hot chilli powder

8 small soft wheat tortillas

150g (5oz) mature vegetarian cheddar cheese, grated

olive oil for drizzling

200g (7oz) can refried beans

1 red onion, chopped

2 tomatoes, chopped

1 Pre-heat the oven to 200°C/400°F/gas 6.
2 Place the beans, avocado, lime juice, 3 tbsp soured cream and chilli powder into a food processor. Pulse until fairly smooth.
3 Spoon a line of mixture just off centre across each tortilla. Roll up the tortillas and put them in an ovenproof dish.
4 Scatter the cheese over the top. Drizzle with a little olive oil and bake for 15 minutes.
5 Heat the refried beans in a small pan. Mix the chopped onion and tomato together to make a salad.
Serve 2 tortillas per portion, with a good dollop of soured cream on top and the refried beans and salad on the side.

Tip You may come across mixed pulses rather than mixed beans. Both are good to use.

crispy potato skins with guacamole

30 mins

serves 4

4 large baking potatoes

1 large ripe avocado

½ onion, roughly chopped

1 garlic clove, crushed

juice of ½ lemon

100g (3½oz) soured cream

2 tbsp mayonnaise

¼ tsp chilli powder

1 green chilli, deseeded

salt and black pepper

1 large tomato, quartered, deseeded and chopped

vegetable oil for deep frying

coarse sea salt, to serve

1 Cook the potatoes in their skins in a pan of boiling water for 20 minutes. Drain.

2 Meanwhile, to make the guacamole, peel and stone the avocado and put the flesh in a food processor with the onion, garlic, lemon juice, soured cream, mayonnaise, chilli powder and green chilli. Season to taste and blend the mixture until it is as coarse or smooth as you want. Then fold in the tomato.

3 When cool enough to handle, cut the potatoes into 6 to 8 wedges. Scoop out the centre of each, leaving a 1cm (½in) thick shell.

4 Heat the oil in a large saucepan and deep-fry the potato wedges for 5 minutes or until crisp and golden. Remove with a slotted spoon and drain on kitchen paper.

Serve the potato skins hot, sprinkled with the coarse sea salt and accompanied by the freshly made guacamole.

30 mins

moroccan chickpea stew

serves 4

400g (14oz) can chickpeas, drained

4 tbsp olive oil

2 red onions, sliced

2 garlic cloves, crushed

1 tsp ground turmeric

1 tsp ground ginger

1 tsp ground cumin

½ tsp ground cinnamon

2 beefsteak tomatoes, chopped

2 sprigs of thyme

2 dried red chillies

600ml (20fl oz) vegetable stock

115g (4oz) cooked rice

2 tbsp chopped fresh coriander

chilli sauce and pitta bread, to serve

1 Heat the oil in a large sauté pan or saucepan and fry the onion, garlic and spices for 5 minutes until the onion and garlic are soft.

2 Add the tomatoes, chickpeas, thyme, chillies and stock. Cover and simmer gently for 20 minutes.

3 Stir in the rice and coriander.

Serve with a good dollop of chilli sauce and some warm pitta bread.

Tip If you like your food extra hot and spicy, why don't you serve this topped with the fiery traditional Moroccan chilli paste, harissa?

20 mins

spicy potatoes with yoghurt & coriander

serves 4

500g (1lb 2oz) potatoes, thickly sliced

400ml (14fl oz) carton natural yoghurt

4 tbsp coarsely chopped fresh coriander

2 tbsp vegetable oil

25g (1oz) butter

1 tsp cumin seeds

½ tsp chilli powder

1 tsp caraway seeds

½ tsp garam masala

salt and pepper

2 tsp paprika

1 Bring a large pan of salted water to the boil and add the potatoes. Boil for 7-8 minutes until the potatoes are just tender. Drain and set aside.

2 Heat the oil and butter in a large frying-pan. Add the cumin seeds, chilli powder, caraway seeds and garam masala and cook for 2-3 minutes until the spices start to release their aromas.

3 Add the drained potatoes to the frying-pan and fry for 4-5 minutes until they are golden and tender. Season well.

4 Either leave the potatoes in the frying-pan or pile them into a warmed serving dish.

Serve the potatoes with the natural yoghurt poured over them, sprinkled with paprika and coriander.

index of recipes

index

acknowledgements

Prelim photography by Sian Irvine.
Title page illustration by Robert Hook.

Photographs: Anthony Blake Photo Library 215, (Sian Irvine) 55, 129, (Graham Kirk) 76, (Joff Lee) 28, 48, 54, 57, 60, 85, 95, 102, 118, 128, 136, 170, 178, 190, 207, (Milk Marque) 148, 154, 171, (Joy Skipper) 46, (Andrew Sydenham) 143, 191, (Philip Wilkins) 112, 147, 219; Eaglemoss Publications 133, 134, 135, 189, (Karl Adamson) 16, 78, 140, 141, 142, 144, 161, 167, 216, (Iain Bagwell) 64, 91, 92, 105, (Ken Field) 14, 33, 138, 205, (Sian Irvine) 10-11, 44-45, 86-87, 106, 123-124, 180-181, (William Lingwood) 20, 26, 35, 36, 50, 59, 61, 97, 99, 113, 124, 146, 149, 150, 182, 192, 198, (Thomas Odulate) 37, 66, 172, 212; IPC Magazines (Marie-Louise Avery/HI) 27, (Iain Bagwell/Living Etc) 82, (Steve Baxter/E) 67, 184, (Steve Baxter/IH) 56, 206, 208, (Steve Baxter/WH) 15, 18, 34, 58, 72, 126, 127, 159, 173, 188, 203, (Chris Bayley/HI) 17, 93, (Peter Cassidy/E) 107, 169, (Peter Cassidy/IH) 162,

(Peter Cassidy/WJ) 94, (Jean Cazals/FC) 52, (Jean Cazals/HG) 104, (Essentials) 153, (Laurie Evans/IH) 96, (Chris Everard/HI) 23, 32, (Chris Everard/IH) 42, 156, 194, (Family Circle) 179, 214, (Ken Field/E) 75, (Gus Filgate/IH) 157, (Michelle Garrett/Op) 151, (Georgia Glynn Smith/HG) 177, (Jeremy Hopley/HI) 90, (Janine Hosegood/HI) 139, 185, (Tif Hunter/WJ) 53, (Graham Kirk/IH) 49, (Nigel James/WH) 199, (Sandra Lane/Op) 29, 38, 39, 40, (Sandra Lane/WH) 74, (William Lingwood/WH) 30, (James Merrell/Op) 81, 155, (Diana Miller/Op) 51, (D Munns/E) 98, (James Murphy/IH) 152, (Thomas Odulate/E) 131, (Thomas Odulate/FC) 24, 137, 166, (Options) 19, (Debbie Patterson/FC) 193, 202, (Bill Reavell/E) 103, 160, 200, (Bill Reavell/HI) 121, 176, 210, 217, (Bill Reavell/IH) 21, 47, 73, 89, 130, (Simon Smith/HI) 13, 204, (Roger Stowell/E) 80, (Roger Stowell/IH) 175, (Sam Stowell/IH) 41, 145, (Sam Stowell/WH) 115, (Ian Wallace/IH) 63, 65, 109, 110, 218, (Ian Wallace/Op) 79, 174, (Philip Webb/FC) 201, (Frank Weider/E) 43, (Frank Weider/HI) 31,

120, 183, (Robert White/IH) 197, (Simon Whitmore/WH) 68, (Paul Williams/WH) 62; Reader's Digest (30 Minute Cookbook/Martin Brigdale) 195, (30 Minute Cookbook/Gus Filgate) 111, 125, 211, (30 Minute Cookbook/James Murphy) 158, (30 Minute Cookbook/Peter Myers) 22, 168, 209, (Low Fat No Fat /Gus Filgate) 12, 25, 70, 77, 83, 88, 100, 101, 108, 114, 164, 165, 186, 187, 196, 213, (Low Fat No Fat/William Lingwood) 71, 116, 117, (Low Fat No Fat/Simon Smith) 84, 119, 132; Elizabeth Whiting & Associates (David Giles) 163, (Brian Harrison) 69.

Illustrations: Robert Hook

Key: E=Essentials, FC=Family Circle, HG=Homes & Gardens, HI=Homes & Ideas, IH = Ideal Home, Op=Options, WH=Woman & Home, WJ=Woman's Journal.